Apple Training Series:

Mac OS X
Deployment v10.6

**A Guide to Deploying and Maintaining
Mac OS X v10.6 Snow Leopard Systems
and Software**

Student Workbook

Apple Training Series: Mac OS X Deployment v10.6 Student Workbook
Courseware Version 10.6.1
November 20, 2009

Published by Peachpit Press
Peachpit Press is a division of Pearson Education.
Copyright © 2010 by Apple Inc.

Apple Training Series Editor: Rebecca Freed
Project Lead/Development Editor: Kevin White
Production Editor: Danielle Foster
Contributor: Simon Wheatley
Apple Editor: John Signa
Technical Editor: Paul Suh
Copyeditor: Corbin Collins
Proofreader: Susan Nasol
Compositor: Danielle Foster
Cover Illustration: Kent Oberheu
Cover Production: Happenstance Type-O-Rama
Interior Design: Danielle Foster

Notice of Rights

Trademarks

ISBN 13: 978-0-321-68048-8
ISBN 10: 0-321-68048-0
9 8 7 6 5 4 3 2 1
Printed and bound in the United States of America

Contents

1   Deployment Planning

1.1	Deployment Concepts.	2
Exercise 1.1.1	Configure the Server Computer.	3
Exercise 1.1.2	Complete the Server Configuration	12
Exercise 1.1.3	Configure the Client Computer	15
Exercise 1.1.4	Install Apple Remote Desktop 3 on the Server Computer	19
Exercise 1.1.5	Use ARD to Control Remote Computers	21
1.2	Deployment Planning	26
Exercise 1.2.1	Automate Asset Tracking with ARD	34
Exercise 1.2.2	Set Up a Server Share for File Storage.	40
Exercise 1.2.3	Use a Deployment Planning Template.	49
Exercise 1.2.4	Create a Deployment Plan (optional)	50

2   Deploying Individual Items and Containers

2.1	Deploying Individual Items	56
Exercise 2.1.1	Use Archiving Tools	62
Exercise 2.1.2	Use ARD to Deploy Items.	71
Exercise 2.1.3	Update Your Deployment Planning Template	73
2.2	Deploying with Disk Images	74
Exercise 2.2.1	Create Disk Images.	80
Exercise 2.2.2	Add a Backdrop to a Disk Image.	84

Contents

Exercise 2.2.3 Create an Internet-Enabled Disk Image 87

Exercise 2.2.4 Segment a Disk Image (optional) 90

Exercise 2.2.5 Use Disk Utility Advanced Settings (optional) . . . 92

Exercise 2.2.6 Update Your Deployment
Planning Template 98

3 Deploying with Installation Packages

3.1 Installation Package Creation 100

Exercise 3.1.1 Create a Basic Installation Package 106

Exercise 3.1.2 Create a Custom Installation Metapackage 112

Exercise 3.1.3 Create a Flat Installation Package 123

3.2 Installation Package Features
and Deployment 125

Exercise 3.2.1 Create an Installation Package with Scripts 132

Exercise 3.2.2 Create a Payload-Free Installation Package 136

Exercise 3.2.3 Create a Snapshot Installation Package 141

Exercise 3.2.4 Install an Installation Package on
a Remote Computer 144

Exercise 3.2.5 Update Your Deployment
Planning Template 148

4 Creating System Images

4.1 System Customization and
Cloned System Images 150

Exercise 4.1.1 Customize Client Settings 159

Exercise 4.1.2 Create a System Image from a Client 168

4.2 System Image Utility and
Modular System Images 172

Exercise 4.2.1 Build a Modular NetRestore Image Using SIU . . . 177

Exercise 4.2.2 Create a Cloned NetRestore Image Using SIU
(optional) 187

Exercise 4.2.3 Update Your Deployment
Planning Template 189

5   Deploying System Images

5.1   System Deployment Overview 192

Exercise 5.1.1 Use Disk Utility to Restore an Image Locally. . . . 195

5.2   Using the NetBoot Service 198

Exercise 5.2.1 Configure Initial NetBoot Settings 207

Exercise 5.2.2 Enable and Test a NetRestore Image 209

Exercise 5.2.3 Create a Server NetInstall Image (optional) 213

5.3   Deploying Systems with NetRestore
and NetInstall. 215

Exercise 5.3.1 Create a Workflow NetInstall Image 223

Exercise 5.3.2 Enable and Test the NetInstall Image. 228

Exercise 5.3.3 Use NetRestore Images with
Alternative Sources. 232

Exercise 5.3.4 Update Your Deployment
Planning Template 238

6   Postimaging Deployment Considerations

6.1   Postimaging Client Configuration 240

Exercise 6.1.1 Update Client Settings Using ARD 249

Exercise 6.1.2 Configure Automated Scripts. 258

Exercise 6.1.3 Install Packages Automatically From a Server. . . 261

6.2   Postimaging Server Configuration 264

Exercise 6.2.1 Use the Automatic Server Setup System 267

Contents

Exercise 6.2.2   Update Your Deployment
Planning Template 274

7

System Maintenance

7.1   **System Maintenance** 276

Exercise 7.1.1   Use ARD to Monitor Systems 281

Exercise 7.1.2   Integrating ARD with Directory Services 283

7.2   **Using Software Update Server and
Maintenance Tasks** 287

Exercise 7.2.1   Set Up Software Update Server 294

Exercise 7.2.2   Configure Clients to Use Software
Update Server. 297

Exercise 7.2.3   Configure Periodic Maintenance Tasks. 301

Exercise 7.2.4   Update Your Deployment
Planning Template 304

Answer Key 305

1

Deployment Planning

1.1   Deployment Concepts

Exercise 1.1.1   Configure the Server Computer
Exercise 1.1.2   Complete the Server Configuration
Exercise 1.1.3   Configure the Client Computer
Exercise 1.1.4   Install Apple Remote Desktop 3 on the Server Computer
Exercise 1.1.5   Use ARD to Control Remote Computers

1.2   Deployment Planning

Exercise 1.2.1   Automate Asset Tracking with ARD
Exercise 1.2.2   Set Up a Server Share for File Storage
Exercise 1.2.3   Use a Deployment Planning Template
Exercise 1.2.4   Create a Deployment Plan (optional)

1.1 Deployment Concepts

This lesson introduces you to the deployment concepts that you will be learning about throughout the course. The goal here is to give a brief overview of all tasks that you will need to consider when planning your deployment.

The exercises presented in this lesson are not directly tied to these deployment concepts for two reasons. First, all the concepts introduced here will be covered in greater detail in the later lessons of this course. Second, the classroom computers have not been configured beyond having a fresh install of the operating system, so the majority of exercises in this lesson will prepare the classroom computers for later exercises.

In this lesson you will, however, be introduced to the document that ties all of the chapters in this course together to help you create a deployment plan. You will use the Deployment Planning Template, introduced in this lesson, to keep track of the techniques you learn throughout this course. On the final day of this course, you will use the information you gathered in this template to create a complete deployment solution that best fits your needs.

Exercise 1.1.1

Configure the Server Computer

Objectives

- Set up and update the student server in preparation for future exercises
- Create an Open Directory master server

In this exercise you will configure Mac OS X Server v10.6 on your server. You will use this Server computer to create images, scripts, archives, and packages, and to deploy those items to other computers on your network.

Classroom Layout

You will work with two computers to complete the course exercises: a server and a client.

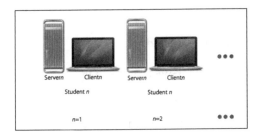

Please remember to perform only those exercises designated for the server on that computer only, and likewise for the client.

Complete Server Setup

Your Server computer should be at the Welcome screen after a successful installation of Mac OS X Server.

> **Note** Ask your instructor to assign you a student number.

1   At the Welcome screen, click Continue.

2   At the Keyboard screen, select your keyboard and then click Continue.

3   At the Serial Number screen, enter the serial number and license information provided by your instructor and then click Continue.

4   At the Transfer an Existing Server screen, accept the default of "Set up a new server" and click Continue.

5   Skip past two Registration screens by clicking Continue on each screen.

6   Select your time zone by clicking on the map and then click Continue.

7   At the Administrator Account screen, use the following information for the Admin account.

   • Name: `Local Administrator`

   • Short Name: `ladmin`

   • Password: `ladmin`

   • Verify: `ladmin`

   • Ensure SSH/remote login is selected.

   • Ensure Enable Remote Management is selected.

8   Click Continue.

9   If the Server Assistant displays an Xsan configuration screen, select "Don't configure Xsan now" and click Continue.

10 In the Network pane, enter the following information to manually configure the Ethernet interface (IPv4) for the classroom environment:

   • IP Address: `10.1.n.1` (where n is your student number)

   • Subnet Mask: `255.255.0.0`

   • Router: `10.1.0.1`

   • DNS Servers: `10.1.0.1`

   • Search Domains: `pretendco.com`

4

11 Switch off IPv6.

12 Select each of the other interfaces (such as AirPort or FireWire) and select Make Service Inactive from the Action menu (the gear on the toolbar).

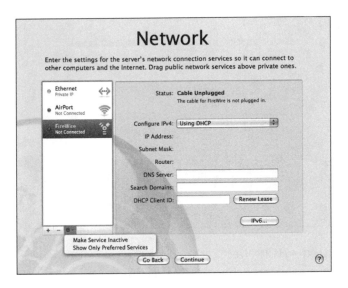

13 Click Continue.

14 For Network Names, verify that your server is using the following names (replacing *n* with your student number):

- Primary DNS Name: server*n*.pretendco.com

- Computer Name: server*n*

15 Click Continue.

16 At the Users and Groups screen, select Configure Manually and click Continue.

17 At the Connect to a Directory Server screen, make sure that the checkbox is deselected and click Continue.

18 At the Directory Services screen, click Continue.

    You will change the Directory Usage settings once your server has been updated.

19 At the Review screen, click the Details button to review and verify the server settings you entered.

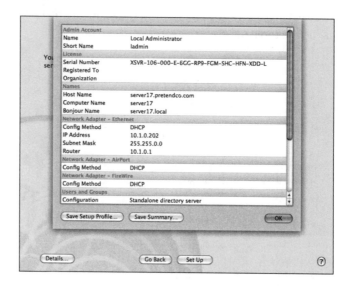

If a setting is incorrect, click Go Back to return to previous screens and make corrections as needed.

20 When you are satisfied that everything is correct, click OK and then click Set Up.

21 Once your server is set up, click the Go button.

Your server should automatically log you in as user ladmin, and Server Admin will open.

22 For the first run of Server Admin, you will need to click the Choose Configured Services button. Do so now.

23 Select the checkboxes next to AFP, NetBoot, Open Directory, Software Update, and Web.

24 Click Save.

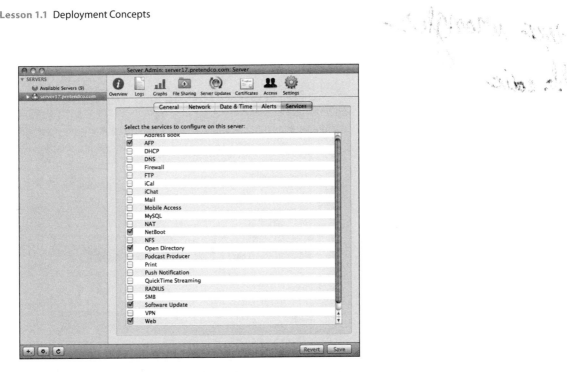

25 Click the disclosure triangle next to your server's entry on the left to show the newly added services.

26 Quit Server Admin.

Copy Student Materials from the Instructor Server

The files you will use throughout this course need to be copied from the instructor's server to yours.

1 In the Finder, use Connect to Server to connect to mainserver. pretendco.com as guest.

2 Mount the Public volume.

3 Copy the Student Materials folder from the Public volume to your desktop.

4 After the folder has been successfully copied, disconnect from the Public volume.

The first set of exercises is complete. This workbook also includes, for your reference, copies of any informational slide shown in class. The next page begins the first set of slides; you can review them now while you wait for your instructor to continue with the presentation.

text wrangler
b.b. edit

Deployment Planning Template

Included in student materials and reference guide

Will complete throughout class

Deployment Planning Template

Chapter 1 – Infrastructure Considerations
Use this template to document any hardware infrastructure considerations that arise during the planning stage of your deployment.

Will your new equipment work within your current power infrastructure?		
Location	**Power Availability**	**Power Requirements**

Will there be any high-performance or high-density situations that require more cooling?

For details, see "Using the Deployment Planning Template" in Chapter 1 of *Apple Training Series: Mac OS X Deployment v10.6.*

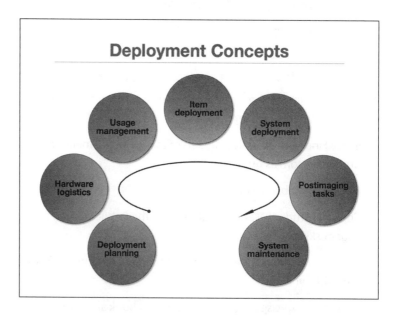

For details, see "Understanding Deployment Concepts" in Chapter 1 of *Apple Training Series: Mac OS X Deployment v10.6.*

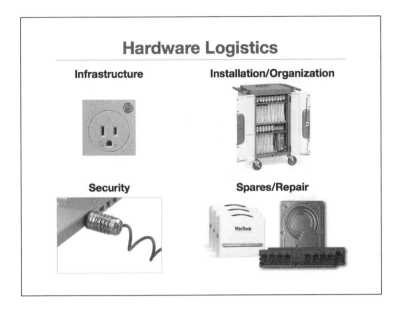

For details, see "Understanding Deployment Concepts" in
Chapter 1 of *Apple Training Series: Mac OS X Deployment v10.6.*

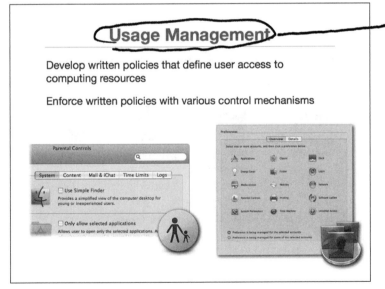

Open Directory
on
our Active Directory
utility.

For details, see "Understanding Deployment Concepts" in
Chapter 1 of *Apple Training Series: Mac OS X Deployment v10.6.*

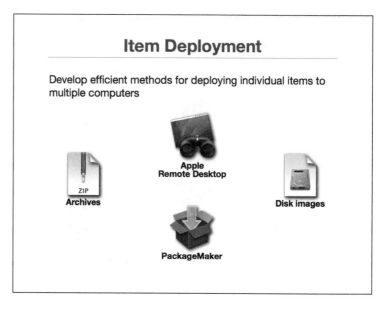

Item Deployment

Develop efficient methods for deploying individual items to multiple computers

Archives

Apple Remote Desktop

Disk images

PackageMaker

For details, see "Understanding Deployment Concepts" in Chapter 1 of *Apple Training Series: Mac OS X Deployment v10.6.*

System Deployment

Deploy entire systems and maintain a uniform computing environment

Disk Utility **NetBoot NetInstall NetRestore** **System Image Utility** **System image Automator actions**

```
hdiutil create -srcfolder source -format UDZO imagename
asr restore --source source --target target
```

For details, see "Understanding Deployment Concepts" in Chapter 1 of *Apple Training Series: Mac OS X Deployment v10.6.*

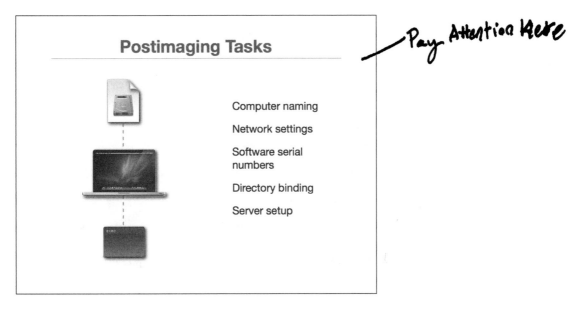

Pay Attention Here

For details, see "Understanding Deployment Concepts" in
Chapter 1 of *Apple Training Series: Mac OS X Deployment v10.6.*

For details, see "Understanding Deployment Concepts" in
Chapter 1 of *Apple Training Series: Mac OS X Deployment v10.6.*

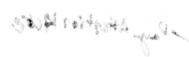

Exercise 1.1.2
Complete the Server Configuration

Objectives

- Install the Xcode developer tools
- Update your server to the latest version of Mac OS X Server
- Configure your server as an Open Directory master

You've just performed the initial configuration of your server. Now you need to install the Xcode tools and any provided Mac OS X Server updates, and configure your server as an Open Directory master.

> **Note** You may find it expeditious to start Exercise 1.1.3 ("Configure the Client Computer") while waiting for Xcode tools and any server updates to complete their installation on your server.

Install the Xcode Developer Tools

The Xcode tools, also known as developer tools, include utilities that will be used in this course.

1   Insert the Mac OS X Server Install DVD in your server's optical drive.

2   Once the media is mounted, navigate to the Other Installs folder on the Mac OS X Server Install DVD to install the Xcode tools.

3   Double-click Xcode.mpkg located in that folder.

4   At the Welcome screen, click Continue.

5   Click Continue and Agree at the License messages.

6   At the Custom Install screen, click Continue to accept the default set of packages to install.

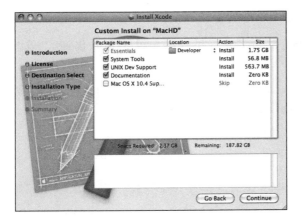

7   Click Install.

8   Authenticate as ladmin when prompted.

9   Click Close when the installation is complete.

Update the Server

Inside the Student Materials folder, you will see the Updates folder. Run the Mac OS X Server updates specified by your instructor.

1   Install any packages that your instructor directs you to install from the Student Materials/Updates folder.

    Updates may be available for the OS and Xcode.

Create an Open Directory Master

Important: The first rule in creating an Open Directory master is to ensure DNS is working properly and your server is responding as expected. Before you configure Mac OS X Server as Open Directory master, it's important to verify network and DNS settings (use the host and changeip commands on the command line to check DNS).

1   On your server, open Server Admin and connect to your server.

2   Select the Open Directory service and then click Settings.

    You can see your server is using a Standalone directory, which is how you set it up in Server Assistant.

3   Click Change to open the Service Configuration Assistant.

4   Select "Set up an Open Directory master" from the list and then click Continue.

5   In the Domain Administrator window, leave the defaults and enter a password of diradmin (the same as the Short Name) and click Continue.

6   View your Kerberos Realm and your Search Base.

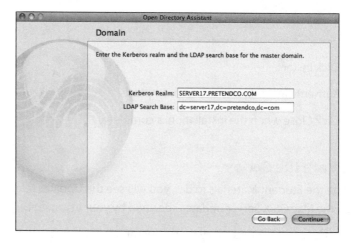

If Kerberos Realm is not SERVER*N*.PRETENDCO.COM and Search Base is not dc=server*n*,dc=pretendco,dc=com (where *n* is your student number), check your DNS settings, and then try again.

7   If everything is correct, click Continue, view the Confirm Settings screen, and click Continue again.

8   Once service configuration has completed, close the Service Configuration Assistant.

9   Verify that LDAP Server, Password Server, and Kerberos are all running by clicking Overview in the toolbar.

If one or more services are not running, use Server Admin to check the Open Directory logs for the inactive service(s) to look for possible reasons for the problem.

Exercise 1.1.3
Configure the Client Computer

Objective

- Use Setup Assistant and System Preferences to set up your client machine

Mac OS X v10.6 should already be installed on your client system but not configured. The computer should be turned on, and the display should show the Welcome screen.

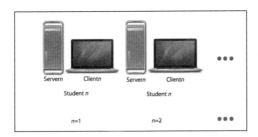

In this exercise you will complete a simple configuration of Mac OS X on your client.

You'll use System Preferences to configure network, sharing, and account settings. You will use the same student number you received from your instructor to provide a unique name for your client.

Configure Basic Settings and Create Initial Administrator Account on Your Client

In this section you'll step through the Mac OS X Setup Assistant to handle initial system configuration for your Client computers.

1   At the Welcome screen, choose the appropriate country and click Continue.

2   Choose the appropriate keyboard layout and click Continue.

3   When asked about transferring information from another Mac, click "Continue to proceed without transferring anything."

4   Verify that Using DHCP is selected for the TCP/IP Connection Type and click Continue.

5   When prompted for an Apple ID, leave both fields empty and click Continue.

6   At the Registration Information screen, press Command-Q to skip the registration process.

7   At the Connect to Mac OS X Server screen, click Continue.

    You will connect to your server later.

8   At the Create Your Account screen, enter the following information:

    - Name: `Client Administrator`

    - Short Name: `cadmin`

    - Password: `cadmin`

    - Verify: `cadmin`

    - Password Hint: <leave blank>

    If your Macintosh includes a built-in iSight camera, you will be prompted with the Select a Picture for this Account screen.

9   Either take a snapshot or choose a picture from the picture library.

10 Click Continue to create the administrator account.

11 At the Select Time Zone screen, click your time zone on the map and then click Continue.

> **Note** Do not click the "Automatic time zone" checkbox.

12 At the Don't Forget to Register screen, click Done.

    The Setup Assistant will quit, and the Finder will open.

13 If you are prompted to install software updates, click Not Now.

> **Note** You will not be required to update your client at this time.

14 Open System Preferences and click Network.

15 Remove all network ports except for Built-In Ethernet by clicking the (–) minus sign for each port (i.e., for AirPort, FireWire, and Bluetooth).

> **Note** Enabling AirPort and connecting to other (public) networks from your Client computer may interfere with future exercises.

16 Click Apply.

Set the Computer Name for Your Client Computer

Because every student has entered the same account name information, all student computers are set to use the same computer name. To distinguish your computer on the network, you need to set a unique computer name.

1 In System Preferences, open the Sharing preference and in the Computer Name field, enter:

`Mac Number` (where *Number* is your student number, spelled out).

For example, student 17 would enter:

`Mac Seventeen`

2 Press the Return key.

Notice that your local host name listed under your computer name is updated to match your new computer name.

3 Click Show All to save the computer name and return to the main System Preferences window.

Bind Your Client Computer to Your Directory Server

In order to use account information supplied by the Open Directory master, you need to bind your Client computer to it.

Directory Utility is used to configure your bindings to other Directory servers:

1   Still in System Preferences, click Accounts.

2   Click Login Options and click the Join button next to Network Account Server.

3   Enter or select your server's DNS name for the server entry and click OK.

4   Authenticate as cadmin (password: cadmin).

    Your Mac OS X computer will contact your Mac OS X Server, locate the shared database, and bind to that server. Several files will be updated and created on your Client computer, allowing it to use the server for authentication. If this process is successful you'll see the message "Server is responding normally."

5   Click OK once more and then authenticate as cadmin (password: cadmin) as necessary.

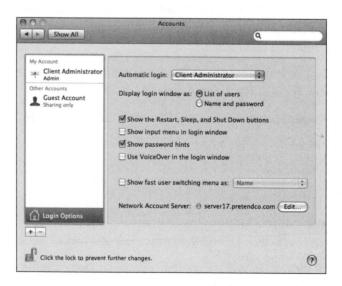

6   Quit System Preferences.

Exercise 1.1.4

Install Apple Remote Desktop 3 on the Server Computer

Objective

- Install and test Apple Remote Desktop (ARD) 3.3

ARD allows you to control, monitor, and generate reports for your computers in the network.

> **Note** This workbook assumes use of ARD v3.3, which was the latest version available at the time of writing.

Installing ARD Admin

You will install ARD on your Server computer and connect it to a Task Server.

1 On your server, navigate to the Chapter1 folder in the Student Materials folder that you copied earlier.

2 Double-click the package RemoteDesktop.mpkg to install it.

3 At the Welcome screen, click Continue.

4 Follow the onscreen instructions to install ARD on the startup volume.

5 Click Install.

6 Authenticate when prompted.

7 Click Close when the installation is complete and unmount the ARD disk image.

8 Repeat the above steps to install any ARD Admin updates that reside in the Student Materials/Updates folder.

9 Add the Remote Desktop application to your Dock and click its icon to open it.

10 At the Remote Desktop Setup screen, enter the serial number provided by your instructor.

11 At the Password screen, set the password to restrict access to ARD and then enter (and verify):

`ladmin`

The password will safeguard this application and any client data associated with it.

12 At the Task Server screen, select "Use remote Task Server," enter `10.1.0.1,` and then click Continue.

13 Authenticate with the Task Server using

User Name: `radmin`

Password: `radmin`

14 Click OK.

15 In the Report Collection screen, leave all the options selected and click Done.

Exercise 1.1.5
Use ARD to Control Remote Computers

Objective

- Control remote clients using Screen Sharing and ARD

In this exercise, you will control your Client computer first with Screen Sharing and then with ARD.

Managing Computers Using Screen Sharing

Use System Preferences to set up your Client computer's screen sharing.

1   On your Client computer, login as cadmin (password: cadmin).

2   Open System Preferences and click Sharing.

3   Enable screen sharing.

    The green status indicator will show that Screen Sharing is now enabled.

    Notice the message that indicates how other users can connect to your computer at vnc://10.1.0.xxx/.

4   Click Computer Settings.

    By default only remote users that authenticate with a local user on this computer may use Screen Sharing. This dialog would be used to grant global access.

5   Click OK.

6   Back on your server, open a new Finder window and select your Client computer under the SHARED heading. (You may need to click All to show all computers on the local network.)

    In the main window, click the Share Screen button under your client's icon to launch the Screen Sharing application (/System/Library/Core Services/).

7   Authenticate as cadmin and observe the window that opens—
    a VNC window showing your client's screen.

8   Try moving a few windows around and watch the effect on
    your client's display.

9   Close the Screen Sharing window.

Enable Remote Management

While Screen Sharing allows users to control their Macintoshes as
if they were sitting in front of them, Remote Management allows
many more features such as copying files, sending UNIX commands, and installing packages from one admin workstation (in
this case, your server). To take advantage of this functionality, you
need to enable remote management on your computer.

1   On your Client computer, open System Preferences and click
    the Sharing icon.

2   Select Remote Management.

3   In the dialog that appears next, hold down the Option key and
    click the first checkbox (Observe). This shortcut will select all
    the checkboxes for "All local users can access this computer to."

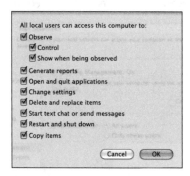

4   Click OK.

    Notice that both Screen Sharing and Remote Management
    cannot be on at the same time.

    Remote Management is now running, and you can now control
    your client from your server running ARD.

5 Back on your server, open Remote Desktop.

6 Click the Scanner entry on the left-hand side.

7 Choose Bonjour from the pop-up menu for your scan.

You should see client (and server) computers listed as they are discovered on the network.

8 Click to select your Client computer and drag it to the All Computers list on the left.

9 When prompted to provide a user name and password, use cadmin (password: cadmin).

The computer is added and ready for you to control.

10 Select the All Computers list and adjust the column sizing so that you can see the ARD version information.

11 If your Client computer reports an older version of ARD than
your server, select your client and choose Manage > Upgrade
Client Software to update it with the server's version of ARD.

Once your client has been updated, select the All Computers
list once more.

Your client should report the same up-to-date version of ARD.

Notice how mainserver is also listed because you are using it as
a Task Server.

12 Select your client and then click the Control button in the toolbar.

You now can control your computer in much the same way that
you did with Screen Sharing.

13 Close the Control window.

14 Click the All Computers list and select your client.

15 Click the UNIX button in the toolbar to send a UNIX command.

16 In the command window enter the following:

```
systemsetup -setcomputersleep Never
```

17 Select User for "Run command as" and in the user box enter:

```
root
```

You are instructing your server to issue the systemsetup
command (using sudo) to your client.

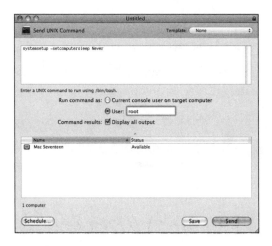

18 Click Send.

19 On your Client computer observe the Energy Saver settings that have now been changed.

Investigate the Other Options in Remote Desktop's Interact and Manage Menus (optional)

Take a few moments to explore some of the other interactive options within ARD.

From the Interact menu you can lock or share a Client computer's screen. From the Manage menu, you can put a client to sleep, wake it, or restart it.

1 Use the Manage menu to restart your Client computer.

2 Use the Interact menu to lock one of your clients, and then unlock it again.

You can take advantage of a wide variety of management options with ARD. We'll see some of the other features later. For now, make sure your client is booted, logged in, and not screen-locked.

1.2   Deployment Planning

When planning your deployment solution, you must consider hardware logistics, usage management, deployment testing, and possibly a service-level agreement. These planning concepts, though not specific to Mac OS X deployment, are fundamental parts of any complete deployment solution. In this section you will explore specific issues related to these planning concepts as they relate to system deployment.

Because the focus of this lesson is overall planning, not all the exercises presented here are directly tied to these concepts. However, you will be using ARD to gather important information about your classroom hardware, and you'll be laying the groundwork for future asset tracking exercises using ARD.

Throughout this course you will experiment with various deployment techniques, but many of these techniques are better served in later chapters.

Power Requirements

amps=watts/volts

Check the Apple "tech specs" pages for power usage information.

Be mindful of rated (often max) vs. real-world power draw.

For details, see "Planning Hardware Logistics" in Chapter 1 of *Apple Training Series: Mac OS X Deployment v10.6.*

Cooling Requirements

Cooling Needs

▶ Know the thermal output of your computers

▶ Know the thermal output of other equipment

▶ Know the capabilities of your cooling system

▶ Plan for worst case

▶ Plan to monitor temperature

General Rule

▶ For every amp dedicated to powering the equipment, another amp should be dedicated for cooling it down

For details, see "Planning Hardware Logistics" in Chapter 1 of *Apple Training Series: Mac OS X Deployment v10.6.*

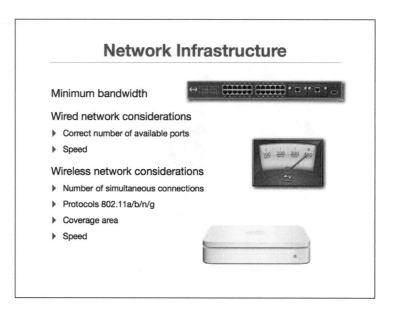

For details, see "Planning Hardware Logistics" in Chapter 1 of
Apple Training Series: Mac OS X Deployment v10.6.

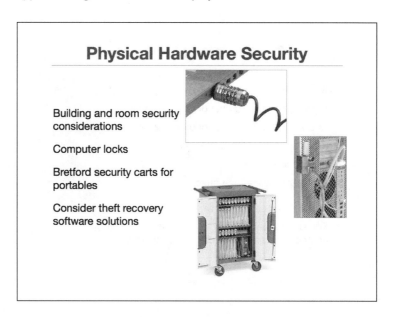

For details, see "Planning Hardware Logistics" in Chapter 1 of
Apple Training Series: Mac OS X Deployment v10.6.

For details, see "Planning Hardware Logistics" in Chapter 1 of
Apple Training Series: Mac OS X Deployment v10.6.

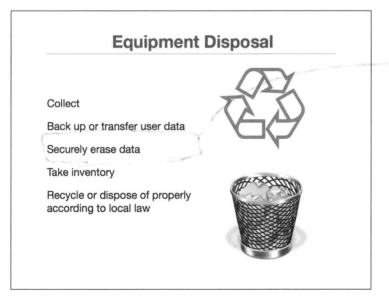

For details, see "Planning Hardware Logistics" in Chapter 1 of
Apple Training Series: Mac OS X Deployment v10.6.

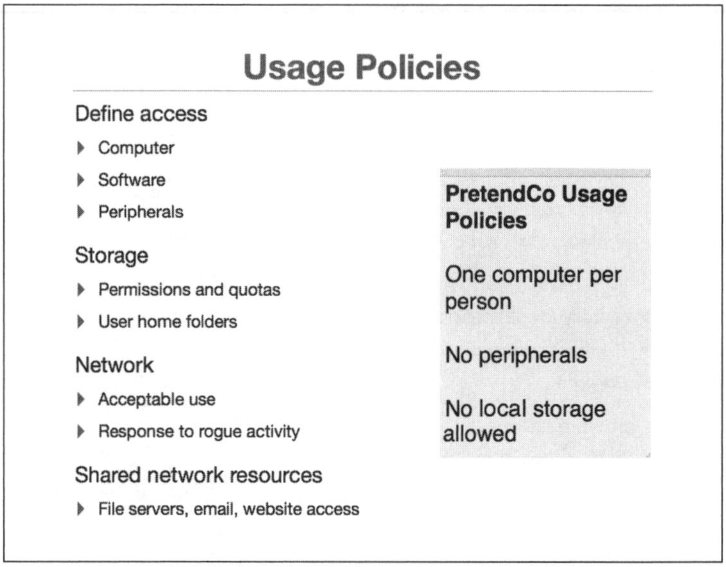

Usage Policies

Define access
- ▸ Computer
- ▸ Software
- ▸ Peripherals

Storage
- ▸ Permissions and quotas
- ▸ User home folders

Network
- ▸ Acceptable use
- ▸ Response to rogue activity

Shared network resources
- ▸ File servers, email, website access

PretendCo Usage Policies

One computer per person

No peripherals

No local storage allowed

For details, see "Planning Usage Management" in Chapter 1 of *Apple Training Series: Mac OS X Deployment v10.6.*

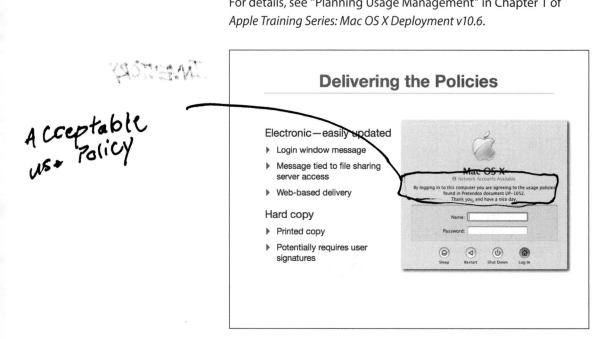

Delivering the Policies

Electronic—easily updated
- ▸ Login window message
- ▸ Message tied to file sharing server access
- ▸ Web-based delivery

Hard copy
- ▸ Printed copy
- ▸ Potentially requires user signatures

Acceptable use Policy (handwritten annotation)

For details, see "Planning Usage Management" in Chapter 1 of *Apple Training Series: Mac OS X Deployment v10.6.*

Enforcing Policies Locally

Consider account types

▶ Administrators

▶ Standard

▶ Limited with management

Home folder location

▶ Default local directory in /Users

▶ Autoerasing (guest account)

▶ External hard drive

Further control access

▶ Restrict with file system permissions

▶ Modify /etc/authorization

▶ Modify /etc/sudoers

For details, see "Planning Usage Management" in Chapter 1 of
Apple Training Series: Mac OS X Deployment v10.6.

Mac OS X Managed Preferences

Directory services–based

▶ Manage via local node

▶ Manage via network directory

Manage at different levels

▶ Users and groups

▶ Computers and computer groups

Enforce usage policy

▶ Configure system settings

▶ Restrict access to resources

▶ Manage home folder content

▶ Manage custom settings

For details, see "Planning Usage Management" in Chapter 1 of
Apple Training Series: Mac OS X Deployment v10.6.

Testing with a Click Matrix

Example task: Open a Pages document and save it to the user's Documents folder.

	Local	Network	Network (mobile)
Base OS	☐	☑	☐
Custom OS— Dept1	☑	☐	☑
Custom OS— Dept2	☑	☑	☑

Action required: Investigate why network Home does not work

For details, see "Developing a Test Plan" in Chapter 1 of *Apple Training Series: Mac OS X Deployment v10.6.*

Network and Server Testing

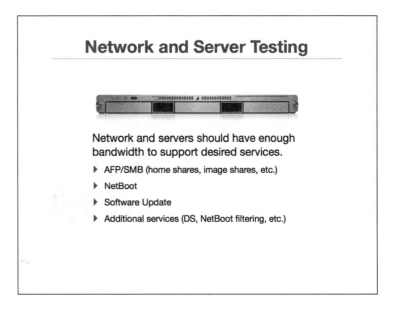

Network and servers should have enough bandwidth to support desired services.

▶ AFP/SMB (home shares, image shares, etc.)
▶ NetBoot
▶ Software Update
▶ Additional services (DS, NetBoot filtering, etc.)

For details, see "Developing a Test Plan" in Chapter 1 of *Apple Training Series: Mac OS X Deployment v10.6.*

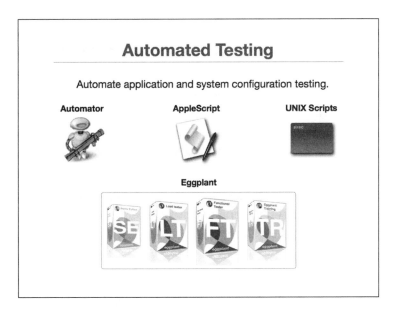

For details, see "Developing a Test Plan" in Chapter 1 of
Apple Training Series: Mac OS X Deployment v10.6.

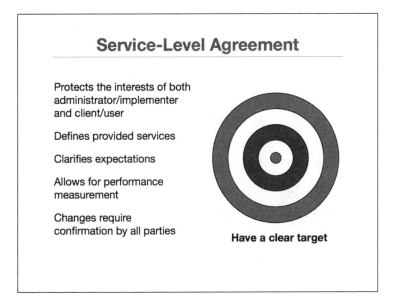

For details, see "Developing a Service-Level Agreement" in
Chapter 1 of *Apple Training Series: Mac OS X Deployment v10.6.*

Exercise 1.2.1

Automate Asset Tracking with ARD

Objective

- Use the reporting feature in ARD to collect information about client computers

In this exercise, you will configure Remote Desktop to store client data on a Task Server for reporting purposes and run several reports using that Task Server.

Connecting to Your Task Server

To speed up reporting, ARD uses a database of client system and file information. You can automate and centralize the collection of this data for reports and determine where the database will reside. In this course, the database is stored on the instructor's server.

1 On your server, open the Remote Desktop application and choose Remote Desktop > Preferences.

2 Click the Task Server icon in the toolbar and verify that the instructor's server is set as the remote Task Server.

3 Click the Reporting icon in the toolbar.

4 Verify that all reporting options are selected and set the reporting time to 7:00 a.m.

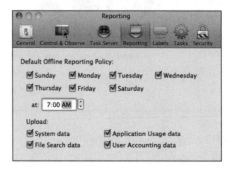

5 Close the Preferences window.

Asset Tracking and Prerollout Reporting with ARD

You will now use ARD to generate reports for the computers in your group.

1   In Remote Desktop, select the All Computers list.

2   Select your client and choose File > New List from Selection.

3   Name your list `lab1`.

    Remote Desktop allows you to have multiple lists of the same name; it does not check for duplicate computer list names.

4   Select your client from the lab1 list.

5   Choose Report > System Overview.

6   In the Categories window, select the following: Computer, Software, Storage, and Sharing.

7   Under the Computer category, make sure that only the following items are selected: Boot ROM, Bus Clock Speed, CPU Speed, Serial Number, CPU Type, Machine Model, Memory, Empty RAM Slots, and Total RAM Slots.

8   In the Template pop-up menu at the top right, choose Save as Template.

9 Use "Overview *n*.1" as your template name (where *n* is your student number).

Templates are useful for storing frequently used report selections in ARD.

10 Click OK and then click Get Report.

It may take a few seconds for the report information to be gathered from each client.

The report window opens to show you your results.

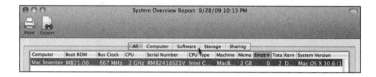

This report can be useful for gathering information about your computers before the deployment of an application or a whole system. You can determine if the computers in the report meet the minimum requirements for the deployment you are planning.

11 Close the report window.

12 Click your lab1 list again and select your client.

13 Choose Report > Network Interfaces.

14 In the Categories window, expand the Network Overview category and make sure that only the following items are selected: Active, Hardware Address, and Interface Name.

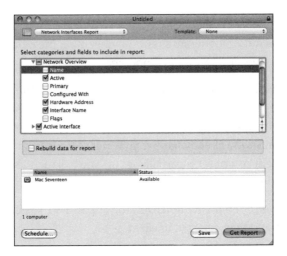

15 Click the top-level checkbox next to Active Interface.

16 In the Template pop-up menu at the top right, select Save as Template.

17 Use "Network *n*.1" as your template name (where *n* is your student number).

18 Click OK and then click Get Report.

This report gives you a summary of the networking information for your computers, including which network interface is active, plus its MAC address.

19 Click the Export button in the toolbar and save this report as a tab-delimited file to your desktop. Accept the default report name given.

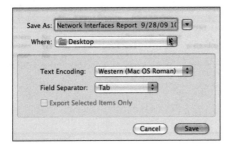

Software Difference Reporting with ARD

You will now use ARD to generate a report highlighting the differences in software versions on your computers.

Normally, you would run an ARD software difference report from a computer (that has ARD installed and configured) with a similar deployment to the other "comparison" computers selected for the report. But because you already have your Server computer set up, and your Client computer is partially set up, you will run the software difference report from your server.

1   On your server, open the Remote Desktop application, select the lab1 list, and then select your client.

2   Choose Report > Software Difference.

3   Select the appropriate checkboxes to include applications in the report and to limit local search to the Applications folder.

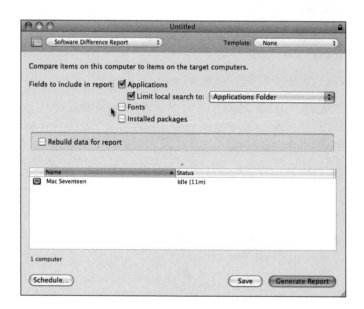

4   Click Generate Report.

> **Note** Software difference report generation may take some time depending on the speed of the computers used in the classroom.

Software differences are highlighted between the server on which you ran this report and the Client computer you highlighted.

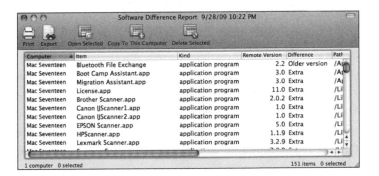

5   Print this report to PDF and save to your desktop as swdiff-*n*.pdf (where *n* is your student number).

You will use this report multiple times to make note of the differences between the application versions on your server and your Client computers—you will use these later.

Exercise 1.2.2
Set Up a Server Share for File Storage

Objectives

- Create a central point of storage for your working files

- Manage preferences for your Client computer

- Create network users with network home folders

In this exercise, you will configure a new Apple Filing Protocol (AFP) share point on your server to serve as a centralized storage location for the files and packages you will distribute to your client. You will also manage a few preferences on your server for your client and, finally, create network-based user accounts. For added portability you will assign a network-based home folder to each network user.

Share a Folder via AFP

You'll share a folder via AFP and set permissions and control connections with Server Admin.

1   On your server open Server Admin and select your server's name. Authenticate if necessary.

2   Click File Sharing in the toolbar.

3   Click the gray Volumes and Browse buttons.

4   Navigate to and select the /Shared Items folder.

5   Click New Folder in the top-right corner of the Server Admin window.

6   Enter `Deployment Library n` (where *n* is your student number) in the name field.

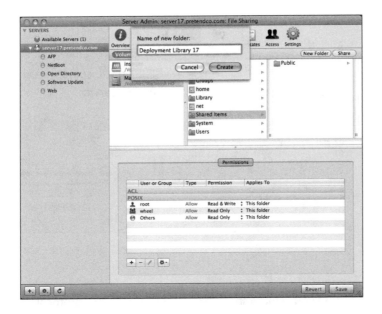

7   Click Create.

8   Select the Deployment Library *n* folder and make sure it is highlighted.

9   Click the Share button and then click Save.

    The item is now shared. By default, Mac OS X Server shares items over AFP and Server Message Block (SMB). Because you want this item to be viewable only by AFP clients, you'll modify the defaults.

10 Click the Share Point tab and then click Protocol Options.

11 In the AFP window, make sure that "Share this item using AFP" is selected (it should be turned on by default).

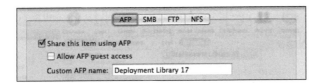

12 Click the SMB tab to show the Windows File Settings.

13 Deselect "Share this item using SMB."

14 Click OK and then click Save.

15 Click the gray Share Points and List buttons.

Your newly shared folder is now visible only to computers and authorized users connecting over the AFP service.

Start the AFP Service

Because you want to share this folder using the AFP protocol, you must configure the service using Server Admin and then start that service.

1 In Server Admin select the AFP service.

2 Click Settings and then click Access.

3 Choose Standard from the Authentication pop-up menu.

4 Verify that "Enable Guest access" is not selected.

5 Click Save.

6 Start the AFP service by clicking Start AFP.

Set Managed Client Settings for Your Client Computer

In preparation for some of the exercises that follow, we will set up a few managed client preferences for your Client computer on your server. You will create a computer group, add a computer to it, and configure a managed preference.

1   On your server, open the Workgroup Manager application,
    connect to server*n*.local (where *n* is your student number),
    and authenticate as ladmin.

2   Once loaded, select your /Lab 1LDAPv3/127.0.0.1 domain
    and then click the lock button and authenticate as diradmin
    (password: diradmin).

3   In the left pane of the window, click the Computer Groups tab.

4   Click the Accounts icon in the toolbar and then click New
    Computer Group in the toolbar.

5   Enter Lab 1 in the Name field (notice how the group short name
    has the space character omitted).

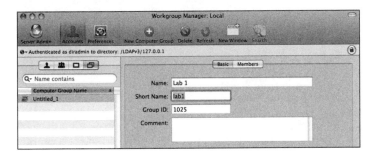

6   Click Save.

7   Click Members and browse for computers by clicking the
    ellipses (…).

8   Select your client and click Add.

    Your Mac OS X Client computer is listed in the browser as Mac
    Number (where *Number* is your student number written out)
    followed by its MAC address.

9   Click Save.

10 Click the Preferences icon in the toolbar and then click the
    Dock icon.

11 Click the Dock Display tab and select Always as the manage-
    ment choice.

12 For the "Position on screen" option, select Left.

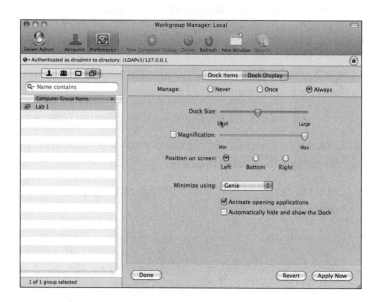

13 Click Apply Now and then click Done.

14 Click Login and then click Options.

15 Select Always as the management choice and select "Computer administrators may refresh or disable management."

16 Click Apply Now and then click Done.

17 Log out of your Client computer and back in as cadmin.

18 Click Allow Settings at the Preferences screen.

> **Note** The Preferences screen appears immediately after login.

19 After you've logged in, notice how your Dock position has changed.

> **Note** The Dock position may not change immediately after the first logout/login or restart.

Optional: Set other computer or computer group–related preferences if time permits. Some suggestions: automatic logout after a time delay, the ability to use the optical drive, and so on.

Managed client preferences are one way to deploy customizations to client computers from a centralized server. In later chapters you will learn other ways to build customizations into a client's operating system.

Create Network Users

In preparation for some of the exercises that follow, you will set up two network users with network home folders. First, you will set up the network-based home folders as automount points.

1   On your server, open the Server Admin application. Select your server's name and then click File Sharing.

2   Click the gray Share Points and List buttons.

3   Select the User's share point and then click the Share Point tab below.

4   Enable automounting for this share point and click OK to accept the default automount options.

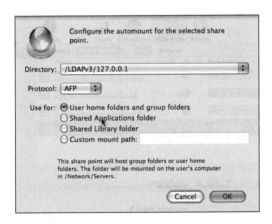

5   In the authentication window, authenticate as diradmin (password: diradmin), click OK, and then click Save.

You have just enabled network-based home folders that can be used by network-based user accounts. You will create two such accounts next.

6   Open the Workgroup Manager application and authenticate as diradmin.

7   Click Accounts in the toolbar and then click Users.

8   Create two new users in the LDAP directory with the following information (replacing *n* with your student number):

- Name: `Mortissia Wells`
- Shortname: `morty`
- Password: `morty`
- Verify: `morty`
- Name: `Client`*n*
- Shortname: `client`*n*
- Password: `client`*n*
- Verify: `client`*n*

Note When you create each user, you may receive a warning that new users may not have access to services. Click OK to bypass the warning.

---

9   Select the two users you just created and click Home.

10 Assign them the following home folder automount of: afp://server*n*.pretendco.com/Users.

11 If the share point does not appear for the user's home folder settings, save your changes, quit Workgroup Manager, and try again.

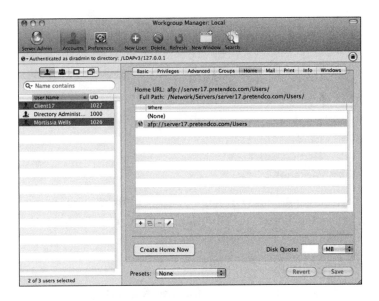

12 Click the Create Home Now button and then click Save.

Set Share Point Ownership and Folder Hierarchy

To organize your work on your server, you need to create a folder
hierarchy that will also be managed by a particular user: client*n*.
(Replace *n* with your student number.)

1 On your server, open Server Admin and select your server.

2 Click File Sharing and select your Deployment Library *n*
share point.

3 Click Permissions and then double-click the owner value (root)
within the POSIX settings.

4 Change the User setting to client*n* with permissions to read
and write.

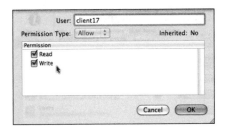

5 Click OK and then click Save.

6 In Server Admin, create the following folders within /Shared Items/Deployment Library *n*/:

- Archives
- Autoinstall
- Images
- Packages

7 In Server Admin, with your Deployment share point still selected, under the Permissions section, select Propagate Permissions from the Action menu.

8 Select all options and click OK.

9 Using the Finder, copy the four new folders to your own (ladmin's) ~/Documents folder.

The folders you copied to your ~/Documents folder will serve as a staging area before you move your work to your Deployment share point.

Now it's time to test connectivity to the share point.

10 On your Client computer, use Connect to Server in the Finder to connect to your server at afp://server*n*.local (where *n* is your student number).

11 Authenticate as client*n* (password: client*n*) and click Connect.

12 Select the Deployment Library *n* volume.

13 Click OK.

14 Verify that the Deployment Library *n* volume is mounted and that you have full access.

15 Unmount the Deployment Library *n* volume.

Exercise 1.2.3
Use a Deployment Planning Template

Objective

- Use a template to capture and document deployment decisions

Use and refer to the Deployment Planning Template throughout the rest of this course.

At appropriate stopping points, add to each relevant section the actions you may need to take during your own deployment using that section's specific deployment method.

The deployment template file is available in Student Materials/ Chapter1; you may ask your instructor for a printed copy.

Exercise 1.2.4

Create a Deployment Plan (optional)

Objectives

- Begin the creation of a deployment plan

- Develop your testing methodology and checklist

- Establish a service-level agreement

> **Note** This exercise is marked optional at this point because you will probably find it best to review these steps after you have completed the entire course. It's simply hard to plan when you don't have a full understanding of all the tools available to you.

Once you have considered the various methods for deploying files, system changes, and complete systems, you should combine those elements you deem necessary into your deployment plan.

At the end of each chapter, you will review and update your Deployment Planning Template. This template can serve as the beginning of your deployment plan.

To complement a deployment plan, two other components are necessary: a test plan and a Service Level Agreement. The former assists in the creation of accurate and error-free deployment mechanisms, whereas the latter ensures that the deployment mechanisms meet some agreed-upon user expectations.

All three components combine to form your deployment strategy. You will investigate the various components here.

Create Your Deployment Plan

Throughout the course chapters, you will be exposed to many deployment techniques and will note those of particular use in your Deployment Planning Template.

The next step is to utilize that knowledge to create a deployment plan based on all the components you want to implement.

At a high level, the delivery methods available to you are:

- Simple file copy
- Centralized copy via Apple Remote Directory (ARD)
- Automated retrieval via scripts
- NetInstall and NetRestore
- Apple Software Restore (ASR) multicast

At a high level, the deployment containers are:

- Archive files
- Disk images
- Installation packages
- System images
- Network Disk Images

Review the methods and containers that you will apply for each of the following events:

- New computer deployment
- New application deployment
- OS update deployment
- Application update deployment
- Regularly scheduled maintenance
- Computer software diagnostics and repair

Create a Testing Methodology for Your Deployment Plan

To effectively and thoroughly test your deployment implementation, you will need to establish your criteria for success and decide how to remedy failures for distinct components.

Testing methodologies may include the following components:

- Discrete testing for Mac OS X components

- Discrete testing for user/custom components

- Discrete testing for Mac OS X application workflows

- Discrete testing for user/custom application workflows

To formalize your progress for each testing category, create a checklist for the objects and steps that you will follow to verify that a mechanism works or does not work.

An example of this checklist, sometimes called a click matrix, is shown below.

Task: Open Keynote.app, create a presentation and save it to ~/Documents			
	Local	**Network**	**Network (Mobile)**
Base OS	n/a	n/a	n/a
Custom OS-Dept1	✓	✕	✓
Custom OS-Dept2	✓	✕	✓
Action Required:	Investigate why network Home folder does not work with Keynote.		

Create a Service-Level Agreement

You will develop a service-level agreement (SLA) that will be used to manage expectations between you and your clients. Using the SLA provided here as a template, you will need to work with your customers and clients to finalize which components of the SLA you plan to include. An SLA specifies what service is to be provided and how it is supported, spelling out details such as response times, service locations, costs borne by each party, performance expectations, and other responsibilities of each party involved.

Developing an SLA helps guarantee that all parties understand the expected outcomes of a system deployment. This document holds both the administrators/implementers and the clients/users responsible for their roles in the deployment. The administrators/implementers will be expected to provide the agreed-upon services—but because there is a set list of requirements, they will not have to keep adding new features at the behest of the clients/users.

Service-level agreements help to manage the following:

- The definition of services
- Performance measurement
- Problem management
- Client/user duties
- Warranties
- Disaster recovery
- Termination of agreement

SLA Template

The [*deployment mechanism*] is used by [*client/customer*] for [*deployment service description*] capability. The [*deployment service group*] guarantees that:

The [*deployment mechanism*] will be available [*insert percentage of the time*] from [*insert normal hours*] of operation (including hours and days of the week). Any individual outage in excess of [*insert time period*] or sum of outages exceeding [*insert time period*] per month will constitute a violation.

[*Insert percentage of service name transactions*] will exhibit [*insert value seconds*] or less response time, defined as the interval from the time the user sends a transaction to the time a visual confirmation of transaction completion is received. Missing the metric for business transactions measured over any business week will constitute a violation.

The [*deployment service group*] will respond to service incidents that affect multiple users (typically more than 10) within [*insert time period*], resolve the problem within [*insert time period*], and update status every [*insert time period*]. Missing any of these metrics on an incident will constitute a violation.

The [*deployment service group*] will respond to service incidents that affect individual users within [*insert time period*], resolve the problem within [*insert time period*], and update status every [*insert time period*]. Missing any of these metrics on an incident will constitute a violation.

The [*deployment service group*] will respond to noncritical inquiries within [*insert time period*], deliver an answer within [*insert time period*], and update status every [*insert time period*]. Missing any of these metrics on an incident will constitute a violation. A noncritical inquiry is defined as a request for information that has no impact on the service quality if not answered or acted upon promptly.

The external availability measurements are done by [*deployment testing team*] and reported on a monthly basis to [*customer/client*]. The internal processes are measured and reported by the [*deployment service group*] to the [*customer/client*] on a monthly basis. This service includes incident reporting.

Typical sections within an SLA:	
A: Statement of intent	This section states the objectives of the document.
B: Approvals: All parties must agree to the SLA	This section contains a list of who approved the SLA.
C: Review dates	This section contains the track record of the SLA reviews.
D: Time and percent conventions	This section contains the descriptions of what time conventions and metrics are being used.
E: About the service	This section introduces the service addressed by the SLA.
F: Description	This section describes the service in detail.
G: User environment	This section describes the architecture and technologies that are used by the consumers of the service.
H: About service availability	This section introduces the availability concepts used in this SLA.
I: Normal service availability schedule	This section describes what is considered normal service availability.
J: Scheduled events that impact service availability	This section describes what scheduled outages are to be expected.

2

Deploying Individual Items and Containers

2.1   Deploying Individual Items

Exercise 2.1.1   Use Archiving Tools

Exercise 2.1.2   Use ARD to Deploy Items

Exercise 2.1.3   Update Your Deployment Planning Template

2.2   Deploying with Disk Images

Exercise 2.2.1   Create Disk Images

Exercise 2.2.2   Add a Backdrop to a Disk Image

Exercise 2.2.3   Create an Internet-Enabled Disk Image

Exercise 2.2.4   Segment a Disk Image (optional)

Exercise 2.2.5   Use Disk Utility Advanced Settings (optional)

Exercise 2.2.6   Update Your Deployment Planning Template

2.1 Deploying Individual Items

At the most basic level, deployment can mean simply the distribution of a few individual items to multiple computers. This lesson focuses on deploying these simple items in a Mac OS X environment. You will first learn about the unique attributes associated with some Mac OS X items, and why you must place those items inside file containers before deployment. This lesson also covers the most basic file container, the ZIP archive file.

Mac OS X File Structure

File System Metadata

▸ Hidden parts of a file that store a variety of resource data

▸ Counterpart is the visible data fork.

Bundles

▸ Folders that group related resources

Packages

▸ Bundles presented in the Finder as single, opaque files

▸ Makes it harder to accidentally delete critical resources

For details, see "Understanding Mac OS X File Management" in Chapter 2 of *Apple Training Series: Mac OS X Deployment v10.6.*

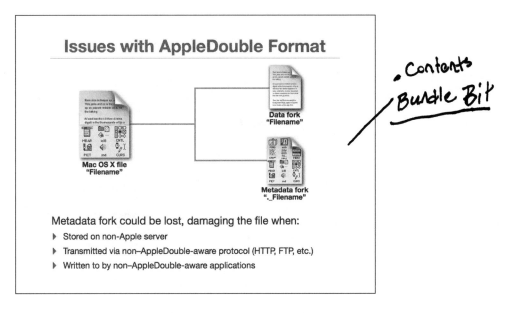

For details, see "Understanding Mac OS X File Management" in Chapter 2 of *Apple Training Series: Mac OS X Deployment v10.6*.

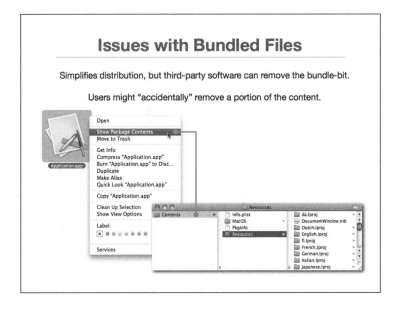

For details, see "Understanding Mac OS X File Management" in Chapter 2 of *Apple Training Series: Mac OS X Deployment v10.6*.

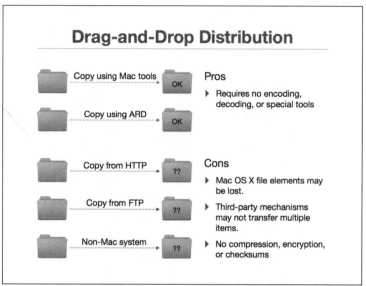

For details, see "Understanding Mac OS X File Management" in Chapter 2 of *Apple Training Series: Mac OS X Deployment v10.6*.

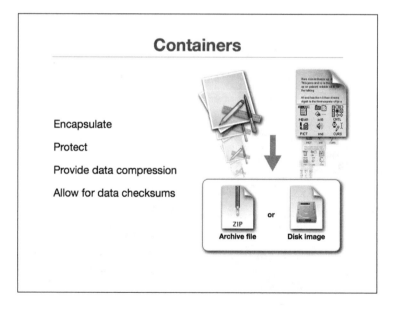

For details, see "Understanding File Containers" in Chapter 2 of *Apple Training Series: Mac OS X Deployment v10.6*.

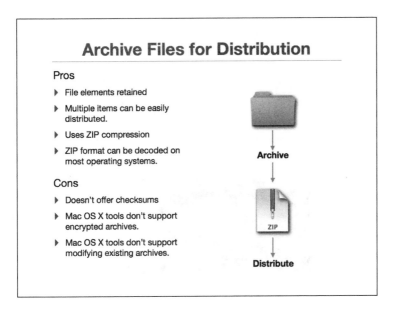

For details, see "Archiving for Deployment" in Chapter 2 of
Apple Training Series: Mac OS X Deployment v10.6.

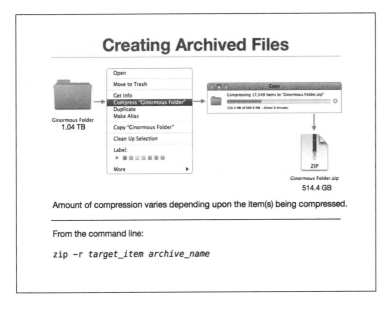

For details, see "Archiving for Deployment" in Chapter 2 of
Apple Training Series: Mac OS X Deployment v10.6.

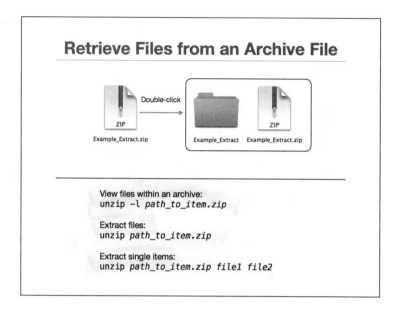

For details, see "Archiving for Deployment" in Chapter 2 of *Apple Training Series: Mac OS X Deployment v10.6.*

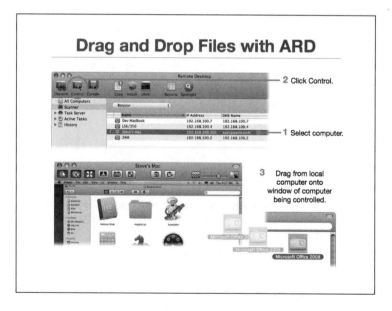

For details, see "Using ARD to Deploy Items" in Chapter 2 of *Apple Training Series: Mac OS X Deployment v10.6.*

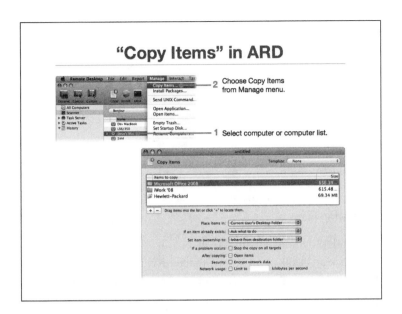

For details, see "Using ARD to Deploy Items" in Chapter 2 of
Apple Training Series: Mac OS X Deployment v10.6.

Zip -p   Target_item
         archive_Node

Exercise 2.1.1
Use Archiving Tools

Objectives

- Use various methods to copy files and configuration settings between client computers

- Use archiving tools to aid preservation of resource forks when copying files

Certain deployment situations call for you to update software or replace an application on one machine with the same version that exists on another. Under these circumstances it may be quicker and easier to perform a direct copy between the two machines. To demonstrate the steps involved, in this exercise you will archive an application bundle on your Server computer, copy it to your deployment share point, and then deploy it to your Client computer.

Copying an Application Bundle to Your Client Computer

You will use the software difference report you generated in Exercise 1.2.1 to identify an application to copy from your Server computer to your Client computer.

> **Note** If there were no software differences highlighted in your report, use the System Image Utility application bundle located in the /Applications/Server folder.

1   On your server, locate the software difference report you saved to the desktop in Exercise 1.2.1.

Lesson 2.1 Deploying Individual Items

2   Review the report and select an application that has different versions on your two computers.

Some example differences reported between Mac OS X v10.6 and Mac OS X v10.6.1 were: Mail, Bluetooth File Exchange, Boot Camp Assistant, and Migration Assistant.

3   In the Finder, navigate to the /Applications folder.

4   Locate the application that you selected from your software difference report.

5   Right-click (or Control-click) on the application and choose Compress "*<application name>*."

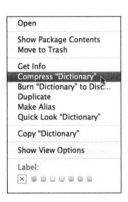

6   Move the newly created ZIP archive to your Deployment Library *n*/Archives folder (authenticate as ladmin as necessary).

7   On your Client computer, connect to your server's Deployment Library *n* share point (authenticate as client*n*).

Replace *n* with your student number.

8   Copy (drag and drop) the ZIP archive from the Deployment Library *n*/Archives share point into the Applications folder on your Client computer.

9   Double-click the archive to uncompress it.

A new copy of the application (with the number 2 appended) is created.

For personal use only. Not for resale.

10 Double-click the newly uncompressed application to verify that it opens.

This is a simple copy of an application from one computer to another. It assumes that the application is self-contained and does not rely on other supporting files to run. Normally, you would update all of your computers with the appropriate software installer.

Copying Files with Metadata, Part 1

You will copy an alias file that you create on your Server computer to your Client computer, via your Deployment Library share point. Instead of using Apple Filing Protocol (AFP) to make the copy, you will use scp on the command line. The scp command is used to securely copy files from one location (source) to another (destination). Either the source or destination can be a local or remote computer. If copying to or from a remote computer, you will need to provide the appropriate login credentials.

1 On your Server computer, navigate to /Applications/Utilities using the Finder.

2 Select the Disk Utility application and press Command-L to make an alias for it.

3 Drag the new alias file to your Deployment Library n/Archives share point.

4 In Server Admin, select your server's entry on the left and click the Access icon in the toolbar.

5 Remove any Service access control lists (ACLs) that exist for the Secure Shell (SSH) service and then click Save.

> **Note** Usually, you would want to leave Service ACLs on to restrict access to the SSH service. As an alternative, you could add clientn to the Service ACL.

Next you will use scp on the Client computer to copy the alias to the desktop on that computer.

6 Copy the alias using scp by entering the following command in Terminal on your client computer:

> **Note** The use of both backslashes and quotes to escape the use of spaces both in the alias name and in the name of your Deployment Library folder on both your client and server is essential.

```
scp clientn@servern.local:"/Shared\ Items/Deployment\
Library\ n/Archives/Disk\ Utility\ alias" ~/Desktop/
```

(*n* is your student number in each case.)

The backslash is also used here as a line continuation character—that is, you can enter this command on two lines, and Terminal will join them up as if typed all on one line.

> **Note** Where possible, tab-completion can help expedite the entering of paths in the command-line interface.

7 Type yes when prompted to exchange keys.

8 Authenticate with client*n*'s password to complete the secure copy.

9 Double-click the alias to open the Disk Utility application.

Question 1 Did Disk Utility open?

_____

_____

10 Drag the alias file to the Trash.

> **Note** scp with the -E option will also copy resource forks.

Copying Files with Metadata, Part 2

You will copy an alias file that you create on your server to your Client computer, via your Deployment Library share point. You will use scp again, but this time you will archive the alias file.

1　On your Server computer, navigate to the /Shared Items/ Deployment Library *n*/Archives folder in the Finder.

2　Locate the alias file you created earlier and right-click it.

3　From the shortcut menu, select Compress "Disk Utility alias."

The file Disk Utility alias.zip is created on your desktop.

4　Copy the newly created ZIP file to the Archives folder on your deployment share point.

5　On your Client computer, copy the zipped alias using scp by entering the following command in Terminal:

```
scp clientn@servern.local:"/Shared\ Items/Deployment\
Library\ n/Archives/Disk\ Utility\ alias.zip" ~/Desktop/
```

(*n* is your student number in each case, and note the use of line continuation characters.)

6   Authenticate with client*n*'s password to complete the
    secure copy.

7   Once the copy is complete, double-click the ZIP archive to
    uncompress the newly copied alias.

8   Double-click the alias to open the Disk Utility application.

Question 2 Did Disk Utility open?

Using the Archive Utility Preferences

In some cases it may make sense to change the default actions
when dealing with archive files. The application that controls these
defaults is called Archive Utility. You will now examine some of the
defaults that this application manages.

1   On your Server computer, open Archive Utility, located in the
    /System/Library/Core Services folder.

2   Choose Archive Utility > Preferences.

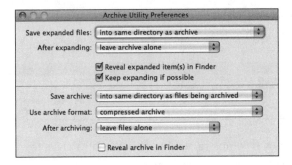

The defaults automate the unpacking of an archive and determine where new archives are created.

3 Examine the options for "After expanding" and "After archiving."

You may consider deleting the original archive once it's expanded to be a viable option. Likewise you may consider deleting the original files once an archive has been created.

4 Close the preference window and quit Archive Utility.

5 To make these preferences readily available within System Preferences, navigate to /System/Library/Core Services/.

6 Control-click Archive Utility and choose Show Package Contents.

7 Double-click Content/Resources/Archives.prefPane.

8 Click Install to add the preference pane for all users of your computer.

Using the Command Line to Archive and Unarchive (optional)

In some situations, it may be more expeditious to use the command-line interface (CLI) to archive or unarchive files.

1 On your Server computer, drag the Disk Utility alias file from your Deployment Library *n*/Archives folder to your desktop.

2 Open Terminal and navigate to your desktop.

3 Execute a "long listing" of your desktop contents:

server17:Desktop ladmin$ `ls -l`

total 2905024

-rw-r--r--@ 1 ladmin staff   171452 Sep 29 00:37
Disk Utility alias

-rw-------   1 ladmin staff   531311 Sep 28 12:36
Mac OS X Server Next Steps.pdf

-rw-r--r--   1 ladmin staff   450 Sep 28 22:17
Network Interfaces Report 9:28:09 10:17 PM.txt

drwxr-xr-x 12 ladmin admin   408 Sep 29 00:55
Student Materials

-rw-r--r--@ 1 ladmin staff 1486436440 Jul 28   2009
Student Materials.zip

-rw-r--r--   1 ladmin staff   51656 Sep 28 22:24
swdiff-17.pdf

Note the size of your alias file using:

`ls -l Disk\ Utility\ alias`

Note the size of your alias file using:

`ls -l Disk\ Utility\ alias/rsrc`

(Both commands should report slightly different sizes as the alias contains both file data and file metadata.)

4 Next, issue the command to archive the "Disk Utility.app alias" file:

`tar -cvf DU-Archive.tar Disk\ Utility\ alias`

The tar command above creates a single file archive called DU-Archive.tar from the Disk Utility alias file.

Avoid using the compress and zip commands as they do not understand file metadata.

5   Next, repeat the long listing of your Desktop folder to see the new archive file details:

server17:Desktop ladmin$ `ls -l`

total 2905704

-rw-r--r-- 1 ladmin   staff   345088 Sep 29   2009 DU-Archive.tar

-rw-r--r--@ 1 ladmin   staff   171452 Sep 29   2009 Disk Utility alias

-rw------- 1 ladmin   staff   531311 Sep 28 12:36 Mac OS X Server Next Steps.pdf

-rw-r--r-- 1 ladmin   staff   450 Sep 28   2009 Network Interfaces Report 9:28:09 10:17 PM.txt

drwxr-xr-x 12 ladmin   admin   408 Sep 29   2009 Student Materials

-rw-r--r--@ 1 ladmin   staff 1486436440 Jul 28   2009 Student Materials.zip

-rw-r--r-- 1 ladmin   staff   51656 Sep 28   2009 swdiff-17.pdf

(You should see that the archive file is larger than the non-zipped alias file because it includes the file metadata.)

6   List the contents of your archive by typing

`tar -tvf DU-Archive.tar`

Notice how there are both resource and data fork files in the archive. The tar command stores the file metadata as an AppleDouble (._) file.

7   Delete your alias file or drag it to the Trash.

8   Next, unarchive to restore your alias file:

`tar -xvf DU-Archive.tar`

You could have also double-clicked the archive file on the desktop to accomplish the same thing.

9   Double-click the alias to test that it still works.

Exercise 2.1.2
Use ARD to Deploy Items

Objective

- Use various methods to copy files and configuration settings between computers

In this exercise, you will use different mechanisms within ARD to copy several files to your Client computer.

Copying via ARD's Drag and Drop

You will copy an ARD software difference report from your Server computer to your Client computer using drag and drop within ARD.

1   On your server, open Remote Desktop and control your client.

2   Using the Finder on your server, drag the software difference report that you saved previously to the screen you are controlling with ARD (the client).

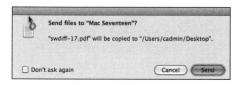

3   Click the Send button to confirm the copy to the remote computer.

4   Close the control window.

5   On your Client computer, examine the desktop.

The software difference report file should now be present.

Copying via ARD's Copy File(s)

This time you will copy a software update file from your server to your client using Copy Files. Once the file is copied, you will control your client and install the update.

1 On your Server computer, open Remote Desktop and select your lab1 computer list.

2 Select your Client computer from the list and choose Manage > Copy Items.

3 Drag and drop the Disk Utility alias you created earlier onto the list of files to copy.

4 Leave the default for "Place items in" as Current User's Desktop Folder.

5 Enable the Open items after copying.

6 Click Copy.

This will copy the Disk Utility alias file to admin's desktop folder and open Disk Utility.

Exercise 2.1.3
Update Your Deployment Planning Template

During previous exercises you copied files manually between one computer and another. Now it's time to update your template to see which of the various methods demonstrated lend themselves to your particular situation:

- Copying nonarchived files between computers using AFP or scp

- Copying archived files between computers using AFP or scp

- Copying files between multiple computers using ARD drag and drop

- Copying files between multiple computers using ARD Copy Files

When filling out your template, please remember to include the rationale for using these forms of deployment.

2.2 Deploying with Disk Images

Disk images are a fundamental Mac OS X deployment technology—to an even greater degree than archive files. With this incredibly versatile container, you can deploy anything from individual items to entire operating systems, all inside a single disk image file. Disk images are one of the two primary tools for Mac-based deployment, the other being installation packages (the topic of Chapter 3).

This lesson provides you with an in-depth understanding of disk image technology, which will provide a foundation for other lessons in this course and very likely for your Mac OS X deployment solution.

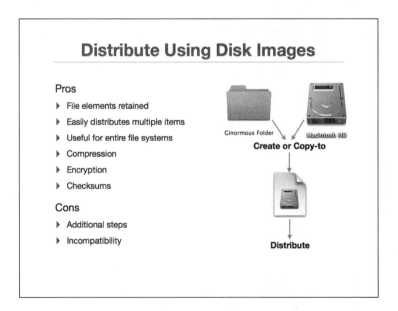

For details, see "Understanding Disk Images" in Chapter 2 of *Apple Training Series: Mac OS X Deployment v10.6.*

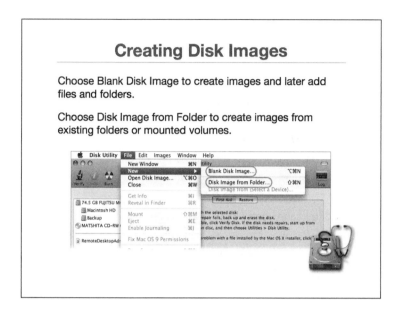

For details, see "General Disk Image Use" in Chapter 2 of *Apple Training Series: Mac OS X Deployment v10.6.*

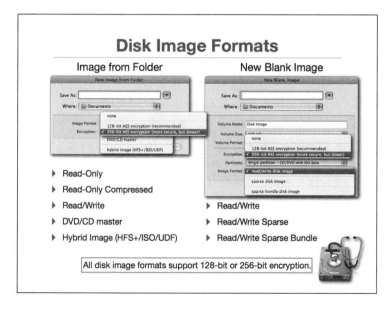

For details, see "General Disk Image Use" in Chapter 2 of *Apple Training Series: Mac OS X Deployment v10.6.*

Read-Only Image Formats

Read-Only and Read-Only Compressed (.dmg)
▶ Contents not editable or erasable
▶ Compressed format can reduce size by 50%.

DVD/CD Master (.cdr/.iso)
▶ Master copies of optical disc volumes; UDF and ISO
▶ Created from other volumes or disk images
▶ Ideal for duplicating media, but less desirable for deployment

Hybrid Image (.dmg/.iso)
▶ Includes volume information in three formats: HFS+, UDF, and ISO
▶ Created from folders or volumes
▶ Good option for deploying to third-party systems

For details, see "Understanding Disk Images" in Chapter 2 of
Apple Training Series: Mac OS X Deployment v10.6.

Read/Write Image Formats

Read/Write (.dmg)
▶ The standard disk image type
▶ Image size set at creation; changeable using management tools

Read/Write Sparse Image (.sparseimage)
▶ Expandable disk image type
▶ Automatically resizes to fit contents
▶ Cannot exceed maximum image size

Read/Write Sparse Bundle (.sparsebundle)
▶ Exclusive to Mac OS X 10.5+
▶ Saved as a package with multiple storage bands
▶ New bands are added as contents increase.
▶ NOTE: Avoid if using for deployment.

For details, see "Understanding Disk Images" in Chapter 2 of
Apple Training Series: Mac OS X Deployment v10.6.

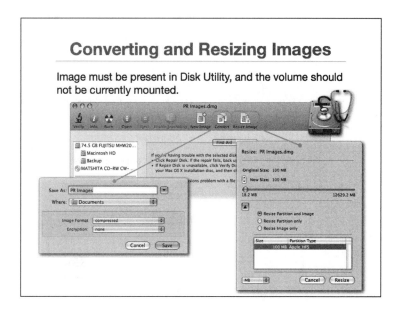

For details, see "General Disk Image Usage" in Chapter 2 of
Apple Training Series: Mac OS X Deployment v10.6.

Using hdiutil

`hdiutil`

▶ Displays list of command verbs

`hdiutil *verb* -help`

▶ Displays documentation specific to command verb

`hdiutil create -format UDZO -srcfolder`
`*path_to_item* *image_name*.dmg`

▶ Creates a compressed disk image from the contents of a folder

`hdiutil segment -o *image_name*.dmg`
`-segmentSize 660m *segmented_name*.dmg`

▶ Segments a large image into files that can fit on a CD (660 MB)

For details, see "General Disk Image Use" in Chapter 2 of
Apple Training Series: Mac OS X Deployment v10.6.

ZIP Archives vs. Disk Images

ZIP Archives	Disk Images
▸ Easier when there are fewer items to deploy	▸ Contents range from simple to complex.
▸ Macs and third-party systems	▸ Deploying entire systems
▸ Novice users	▸ Contents need to be editable.
▸ Quick lossless compression	▸ Compression is optional but not required.
	▸ Encryption
	▸ Data checksums

ZIP

For details, see "Understanding File Containers" in Chapter 2 of *Apple Training Series: Mac OS X Deployment v10.6.*

Customizing Disk Images

Create easy instructions for your users.

PretendCo
deployment services

Custom.app → Applications

drag your update to the Applications folder

For details, see "Using Disk Image Deployment Features" in Chapter 2 of *Apple Training Series: Mac OS X Deployment v10.6.*

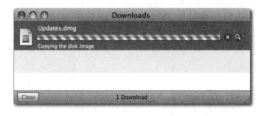

For details, see "Using Disk Image Deployment Features" in Chapter 2 of *Apple Training Series: Mac OS X Deployment v10.6.*

Exercise 2.2.1

Create Disk Images

Objective

- Create various types of disk images using Disk Utility, including encrypted and compressed disk images

You will use Disk Utility to create disk images, resize a disk image to accommodate additional files, and convert the disk image to a different type.

Create and Resize a Disk Image

In this exercise, you will use disk images to copy updated applications to your Client computer.

1   On your Server computer, locate your software difference report and choose an application that is greater than 40 MB in size and that the report shows as an older version on the client.

    The Mail application is a good choice here.

2   Open Disk Utility in /Applications/Utilities.

3   Choose File > New > Blank Disk Image.

4   Name your image

    `p-update-n-yyyy-mm`.dmg

    (where *n* is your student number, *yyyy* is the year, and *mm* is the month).

5   Set the volume name to

    `Pretendco update for MMM yyyy`

    (where *MMM* is the three-letter abbreviation for the month and *yyyy* is the year).

6   Choose to save to the ~/Documents/Archives, and make the size of the disk image 40 MB.

Leave the other default settings.

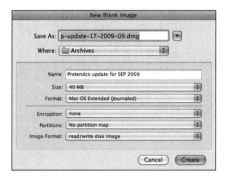

7   Click Create.

Disk Utility will create a new disk image and automatically mount it on your desktop.

8   Drag the application that you selected previously onto the new mounted disk image volume.

You should see a message indicating that there is not enough free space on your disk volume.

9   Click OK to dismiss the dialog.

10 In Disk Utility, eject your volume by clicking the Eject icon in the toolbar.

11 Click the Resize Image button in the toolbar, enter a new size of 100 MB, and click Resize.

12 Double-click your disk image from the source list to remount it.

13 Attempt to copy the application to your newly resized disk volume again.

Question 3 Did the copy succeed?

14 Unmount your disk image.

Compress and Encrypt Your Disk Image

To save space and time during disk image transfers, and to provide security during transit, you will now compress and encrypt the disk image you created previously.

1 Open Disk Utility and select your disk image from the source list.

Make a note of the disk image size from the information at the foot of the Disk Utility window.

Disk Image Size:

> **Note** You may need to remove and re-add the disk image into the source list of Disk Utility in order for the new disk image size to be refreshed.

2 Choose Images > Convert.

3 Leave the name as it is and verify that "compressed" is selected in the Image Format pop-up menu.

4 For the encryption type, choose "128-bit AES."

5   Click Save and then click Replace to replace your existing disk image. When prompted to set an encryption password, use `ladmin`.

> **Note** This is a weak password. You would choose a stronger password that is easy for you to remember but hard for others to guess.

Check the size of the disk image in Disk Utility now.

Question 4 Has the size changed?

6   Remove the disk image from the source list within Disk Utility by dragging it to the desktop.

You will now add the same disk image again so that its size can be reread.

7   Drag the disk image from the ~/Documents/Archives back into the Disk Utility source list.

8   Now record the disk image size.

Disk Image Size:

As it stands, this disk image could be used to deploy the updated application to your client; however, you will make one more change during the next exercise and then deploy it.

Exercise 2.2.2
Add a Backdrop to a Disk Image

Objective

- Create a customized disk image with a background image and alias

In this exercise, you will take the disk image that contains an application (from the previous exercise), add a link to the /Applications folder, and then add a graphical backdrop that provides instructions on how to install the application (drag and drop into the Applications folder). The disk image will be copied to the Deployment Library share point next, and then down to the Client computer.

1 On your server, in the Disk Utility application, select your disk image from the source list and choose Images > Convert from the menu bar.

   You need to make the disk image read-writable instead of compressed in order to make changes.

2 From the appropriate pop-up menus, choose read/write for the format and 128-bit AES for the encryption and then click the Save button.

3 Click the Replace button to replace your existing disk image and use the ladmin credentials when prompted.

4 Click the OK button to convert the disk image.

5 Double-click the disk image to mount the volume on your desktop.

   If prompted by Keychain, click Allow.

6 In the Finder, create an alias for the Applications folder and copy it into the disk image.

7 Rename the copied alias from "Applications alias" to just "Applications."

8 Drag the Student Materials/Chapter2/diskpic.jpg file into your disk image.

9   Select your mounted disk image from the Finder sidebar.

10 Change the disk image Finder view to Icon view.

11 Choose View > Show View Options.

12 Select the Icon size to be 80 by 80 and move the grid spacing slider to the far right.

13 Select Show Icon Preview and choose Snap to Grid from the "Arrange by" pop-up menu.

14 For the Background, select Picture and then double-click the area labeled "Drag image here," and navigate to your disk image to select diskpic.jpg. Or drag and drop the copy of the diskpic.jpg file from the disk image into the area labeled "Drag image here." Close the view options inspector window.

15 Hide diskpic.jpg using these commands in the command line (replace *MMM* with the month and *YYYY* with the year):

```
cd /Volumes/Pretendco\ updates\ for\ MMM\ YYYY/
mv diskpic.jpg .diskpic.jpg
cd
```

Do not miss the final cd command or you will not be able to unmount the disk image in step 17.

16 Back in the Finder, move the icons around the disk image until the updated application and the application alias icons are placed in their indicated boxes.

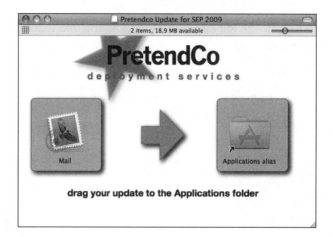

17 Unmount the disk image.

18 Compress and encrypt the disk image with Disk Utility; use a password of "08pcds" and choose to replace the existing disk image.

19 Drag the disk image to your Server's Deployment Library n/Archives share point. (Authenticate as necessary.)

20 On your Client computer, connect to your server's Deployment Library share point.

21 Authenticate as clientn.

22 Copy the disk image to the desktop from the Archives folder on the Deployment Library n share point.

23 Remove the existing copy of the application from the Applications folder. (Authenticate as cadmin.)

24 Double-click the disk image, provide the password, and then follow the instructions displayed in the background image.

You have now updated another application on your Client computer, this time using a disk image as the container.

Exercise 2.2.3
Create an Internet-Enabled Disk Image

Objective

- Create a disk image that automounts and empties its contents for you

In this exercise you will create a disk image that, when opened, copies its contents to the same location in the file system and then moves itself to the Trash.

Start Web Services

To make the disk image available via web services, you will set up basic web services on your server.

1   On your server, open the Server Admin application and then click Web.

2   Click the Sites icon in the toolbar and then select your default website ('*').

3   Click the Options tab and enable Folder Listing for your site.

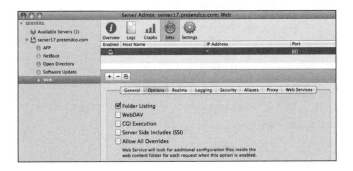

4   Click the Save button and then click the Start Web button to start web services.

5   In the Finder create a new folder called "downloads" within the /Library/WebServer/Documents/ folder; authenticate as ladmin if necessary.

Make Your Disk Image Internet-Enabled

While Internet-enabled disk images are an ideal way to automate delivery of software and files to a Client computer, they need to be checksummed so that Mac OS X can detect whether they have been modified during transit to the client. You will checksum your disk image in preparation to make it Internet-enabled.

1   Use Disk Utility on your server to create a new disk image on your ~/Documents/Archives of 100 MB in size. Name it

    `i-update-`*n*`-`*yyyy*`-`*mm*`.dmg`

    (where *n* is your student number, *yyyy* is the year, and *mm* is the month).

2   Drag the widget /Library/Widgets/Server Status into the new disk image.

3   Unmount the disk image once the widget has been copied.

4   Use Disk Utility to make the new disk image read-only using the Convert feature, replacing the existing disk image.

5   Next, checksum your image by choosing Images > Checksum > CRC-32 image checksum.

6   Verify your image's checksum from the Images menu.

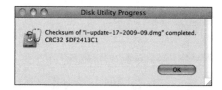

7   Open Terminal and make the disk image Internet-enabled by issuing the command

    `hdiutil internet-enable ~/Documents/Archives/\`
    `i-update-`*n*`-`*yyyy*`-`*mm*`.dmg`

8   Once you see the message "`hdiutil: internet-enable: enable succeeded`" copy the disk image to your Server's /Library/WebServer/Documents/downloads/ folder.

Test the Disk Image on Your Client Computer

Now that you have created an Internet-enabled disk image and posted it on the Server computer's website, download the image onto the client and open it to make sure it opens properly.

1   On your Client computer, open Safari.

2   In Safari Preferences > General, verify that "Open 'safe' files after downloading" is selected.

3   Close Preferences window.

4   Browse to: http://server*n*.local/downloads/.

    A list of files should be displayed in your browser.

5   Click the disk image file to start the download.

    Once the disk image has copied down, the image will mount, the contents will copy to ~/Downloads, and the disk image will move to the Trash.

    Because the newly downloaded file is a widget, the Widget Installer application will launch and prompt you for install confirmation.

6   Click Install.

7   Enter your server's connection information and click Done.

8   To add this widget to your collection on this computer, click Keep.

> **Note** Mac OS X v10.6 will not allow Internet-enabled disk images to unload themselves inside the Applications folder, even when Safari's "Open 'safe' files" option is selected.

Exercise 2.2.4
Segment a Disk Image (optional)

Objective

- Segment a large disk image into smaller segments

In this exercise you will make a large disk image and then use the `hdiutil` command to break it up into two or more smaller disk image segments. The segments will then be copied to the target computer, where the segmented disk image will be opened to verify that the segmentation worked correctly.

1 On your server, reference the software difference report and select an application that you need to update in your Client computer's Applications folder.

2 Use the Disk Utility application to create a new disk image in ~/ Documents/Archives of 100 MB in size. Name it

   `i-update-n-yyyy-mm-2.dmg`

   (where *n* is your student number, *yyyy* is the year, and *mm* is the month).

3 Drag your chosen application into the new disk image.

   If the disk image is not large enough, resize it following the instructions shown in Exercise 2.2.1 under "Create and Resize a Disk Image."

4 Unmount the disk image once the application has been copied.

5 Convert the image to read-only and then save it with the same name to replace the original.

   Only read-only disk images can be segmented.

6 Open Terminal and then segment your disk image using:

   ```
   hdiutil segment -o ~/Documents/Archives/\
   i-update-n-yyyy-mm-2-seg -segmentSize 10m \
   ~/Documents/Archives/i-update-n-yyyy-mm-2.dmg
   ```

Replacing *n*, *yyyy*, and *mm* with your student number, year, and the two-digit number for the month, respectively.

Depending on the size of the application that you put in the disk image, `hdiutil` will create several disk segments.

7   Copy the disk segments to the Archives folder on the Deployment Library share point. (Authenticate as necessary.)

8   On the Client computer, drag and drop to copy the disk image segments from the Deployment Library *n*/Archives folder to the desktop and then double-click the first segment:

`i-update-`*n*`-`*yyyy*`-`*mm*`-2-seg.dmg`

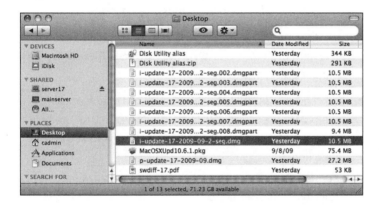

9   After the disk image mounts, drag the updated application contained within it to the /Applications folder. Click Replace when prompted.

Exercise 2.2.5
Use Disk Utility Advanced Settings (optional)

Objectives

- Enable advanced preferences for Disk Utility, including the Debug menu

- Use hdiutil to manipulate disk images at the command line

- Use hdiutil to flatten disk images

Certain disk image manipulation settings are available via additional system preferences and via the way Disk Utility is used. You will explore both options here.

1 You can set Disk Utility to show advanced image options when manipulating existing disk images. Make sure Disk Utility is not running and then issue the following command at the command line:

```
defaults write com.apple.DiskUtility advanced-\
image-options -bool YES
```

2 Open Disk Utility and select one of your disk images from the source list.

3 Choose Images > Checksum and then notice the new checksum options:

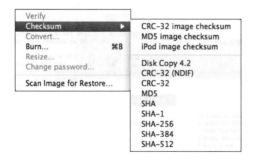

4   Next choose Images > Convert and notice the new image
    format options:

5   Quit Disk Utility without making any changes.

6   To add the Debug menu to Disk Utility, issue the command

```
defaults write com.apple.DiskUtility \
DUDebugMenuEnabled -bool YES
```

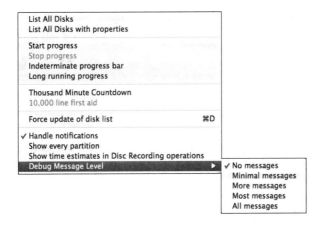

When you run Disk Utility again, a new Debug menu will
be present.

7   To remove either option, write to defaults again with a key
    value of -bool NO.

These changes will take effect the next time you open
Disk Utility.

More hdiutil

In some cases it may be more expeditious to use hdiutil at the command line. In addition, certain operations such as disk segmentation cannot be performed with the Disk Utility GUI application.

1   Navigate to ~/Documents/Archives on your server.

2   Create a disk image of 40 MB in size, HFS+Journaled with the volume name "update3":

```
hdiutil create -size 40m -volname "update3" \
-fs HFS+J i-update3.dmg
```

3   Compress and encrypt the disk image with the following command:

```
echo -n pass | hdiutil convert i-update3.dmg \
-format UDBZ -o i-update3-ce.dmg -encryption \
AES-128 -stdinpass
```

Using hdiutil Checksum and Convert Functions

You will use hdiutil to checksum and verify a disk image in preparation for placing it on the web for download.

1   Create a read-only disk image that is 10 MB in size:

```
hdiutil create -size 10m -volname "update4" \
i-update4.dmg
```

```
hdiutil convert i-update4.dmg -format UDRO -o \
i-update4-ro.dmg
```

2   When creating a read-only disk image, a checksum is automatically calculated. To re-checksum an image, use the following:

```
hdiutil checksum i-update4-ro.dmg -type CRC32
```

3   Checksums can be added to almost all images, but this verification works best on read-only or compressed images:

```
hdiutil verify i-update4-ro.dmg
```

4   To create a read-only disk image from an application / folder
    (such as Automator.app), use the following:

```
hdiutil create -srcfolder /Applications/\
Automator.app -format UDRO otto.dmg
```

You will need to authenticate as ladmin to complete the
operation.

> **Note** Terminal may report an authentication error even
> though the disk image is created successfully.

Using hdiutil flatten with Compression Tools

You will use hdiutil to flatten a disk image that was created with
an earlier version of Mac OS X (one that has file metadata).

1   In Terminal, navigate to Student Materials/Chapter2.

2   Perform a long listing of the folder and check the reported size
    of the disk image named unflattened-one.dmg.

server17:Chapter2 ladmin$ `ls -l`

total 6584

*-rwxrwxrwx 1 ladmin admin   86984 Sep 28 22:39
diskpic.jpg*

*-rw-r--r--@ 1 ladmin admin 3271680 Feb 24   2009
unflattened-one.dmg*

3   In the Finder, open a Get Info window for the same file and
    compare reported sizes.

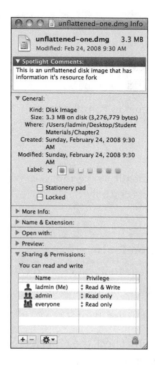

The difference indicates that some information is stored as file metadata for this disk image. Copying this disk image between systems or using protocols that do not understand file metadata will result in data loss, such as the color label for this disk image.

4   In the Finder, make two copies of the unflattened-one.dmg disk image on your desktop and call them fork1a.dmg and fork1b.dmg.

5   In Terminal, navigate to ~/Desktop and flatten the first disk image (embed the resource fork data into the data fork):

```
hdiutil flatten fork1a.dmg
```

Leave fork1b.dmg alone.

6 Next, compress and uncompress both images using a command-line method that does not understand resource forks:

```
compress fork1a.dmg ; uncompress fork1a.dmg.Z
```

Replace the file if prompted.

```
compress fork1b.dmg ; uncompress fork1b.dmg.Z
```

7 Double-click each disk image to mount them both.

Question 5 Which of the disk images still works?

Exercise 2.2.6
Update Your Deployment Planning Template

During the previous exercises you have manipulated disk images using both Disk Utility and the `hdiutil` command. Disk images are particularly useful for encapsulating software updates, packages, and applications for delivery locally or across the Internet.

Now it's time to update your deployment planning template to see which of the various methods demonstrated lend themselves to your particular situation:

- Using disk images with graphics and aliases

- Using Internet-enabled disk images

- Using segmented disk images

- Using compressed disk images with encryption

When you're filling out your template, please remember to include the rationale for using the forms of deployment that you select.

3

Deploying with Installation Packages

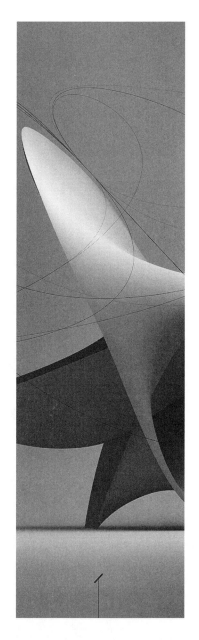

3.1   Installation Package Creation

Exercise 3.1.1   Create a Basic Installation Package

Exercise 3.1.2   Create a Custom Installation Metapackage

Exercise 3.1.3   Create a Flat Installation Package

3.2   Installation Package Features and Deployment

Exercise 3.2.1   Create an Installation Package with Scripts

Exercise 3.2.2   Create a Payload-Free Installation Package

Exercise 3.2.3   Create a Snapshot Installation Package

Exercise 3.2.4   Install an Installation Package on a Remote Computer

Exercise 3.2.5   Update Your Deployment Planning Template

3.1 Installation Package Creation

In addition to disk images, installation packages are the other primary Mac OS X deployment technology. Installation packages provide a powerful solution for deploying complex collections of items in a manner that is professional looking, consistent, and easily audited. As a result, all Apple software and updates are distributed as installation packages. With Mac OS X v10.6 Apple has made creating your own custom installation packages even easier with a completely new version of PackageMaker. In this lesson you will learn how to take advantage of this technology to create custom installers. This knowledge will also provide a foundation for other lessons in this course and very likely for your Mac OS X deployment solution.

Benefits of Installation Packages

Distribute single files
or groups of items

Consistent install behavior

Automation options

Trackable and easily audited

Combine with ARD for a
powerful distribution option

For details, see "Understanding Mac OS X Installation Technology" in Chapter 3 of *Apple Training Series: Mac OS X Deployment v10.6*.

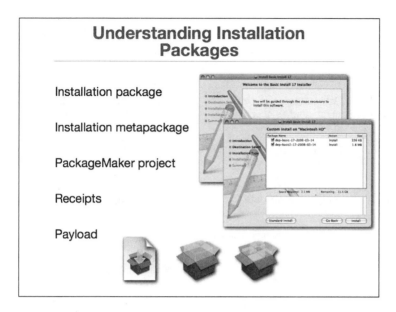

For details, see "Understanding Mac OS X Installation Technology" in Chapter 3 of *Apple Training Series: Mac OS X Deployment v10.6*.

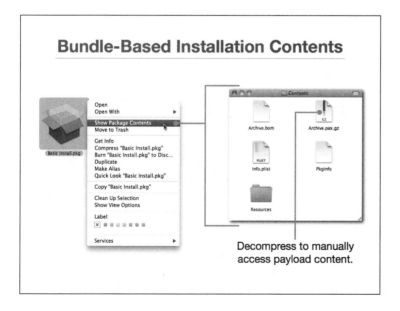

For details, see "Understanding Mac OS X Installation Technology" in Chapter 3 of *Apple Training Series: Mac OS X Deployment v10.6*.

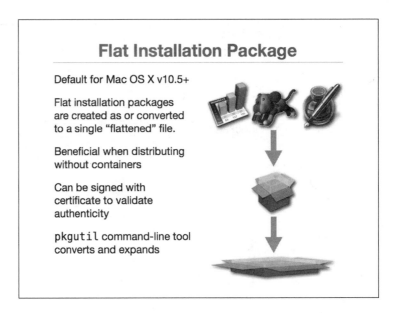

For details, see "Understanding Mac OS X Installation Technology" in Chapter 3 of *Apple Training Series: Mac OS X Deployment v10.6*.

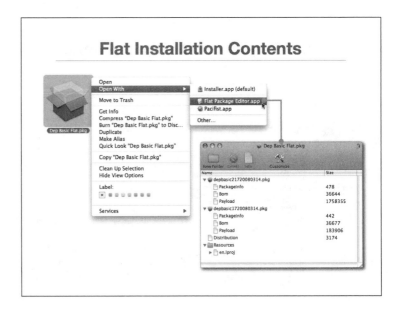

For details, see "Understanding Mac OS X Installation Technology" in Chapter 3 of *Apple Training Series: Mac OS X Deployment v10.6*.

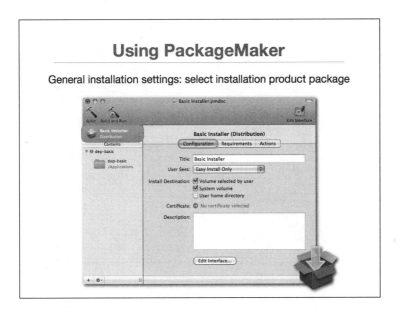

For details, see "Creating Installation Packages" in Chapter 3 of
Apple Training Series: Mac OS X Deployment v10.6.

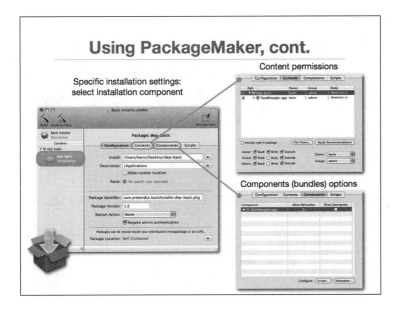

For details, see "Creating Installation Packages" in Chapter 3 of
Apple Training Series: Mac OS X Deployment v10.6.

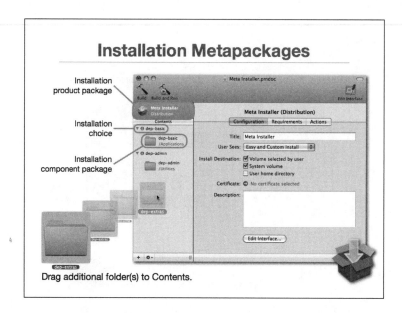

For details, see "Creating Installation Metapackages" in Chapter 3 of *Apple Training Series: Mac OS X Deployment v10.6.*

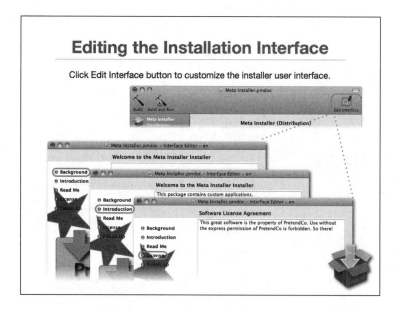

For details, see "Customizing the Installation Interface" in Chapter 3 of *Apple Training Series: Mac OS X Deployment v10.6.*

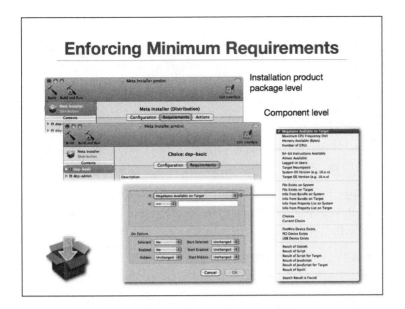

For details, see "Setting Installation Requirements" in Chapter 3 of
Apple Training Series: Mac OS X Deployment v10.6.

Exercise 3.1.1
Create a Basic Installation Package

Objective

- Create an installation package to deliver custom files or folders on a target computer

PackageMaker is delivered with Apple's Xcode developer software. With this application you can create customized installation packages, which will give your users a common experience.

In this exercise you will use a folder hierarchy for managing where the files will be installed on a Client computer and use the PackageMaker utility to make an installation package.

Use PackageMaker to Create a Installation Package

To create an installation package, you select the components in PackageMaker. This should be completed on your Server computer and tested on your Client computer.

1 Log in as ladmin on your Server computer.

2 Open PackageMaker (/Developer/Applications/Utilities).

   Because you'll be using PackageMaker frequently during this chapter, you might consider keeping it in the Dock.

3 At the Install Properties dialog, enter `com.pretendco` for the organization, change the Minimum Target setting to Mac OS X v10.4 Tiger, and click OK.

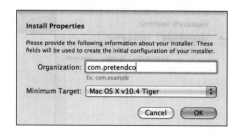

Because you are creating a new project, you need to supply default information.

4 Click the Configuration button and give your new installation package the title of "Basic Install *n*" (where *n* is your student number).

5 For Install Destination, select the "System volume" checkbox only.

You will be adding additional requirements and actions in a later exercise. For now, you'll add the content to your installation package.

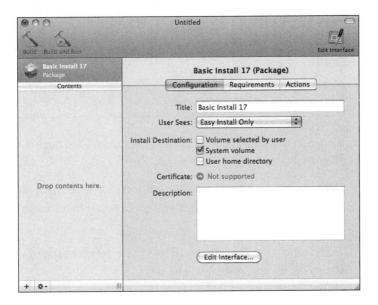

6 Drag the Documentation folder from Student Materials/ Chapter3 into your new installation package contents pane.

7 Select the Documentation component payload (the folder) and click the Configuration button.

8   Change the destination to /Documentation.

Notice how the Configuration screen has been filled out with the installation package identifier.

Because this installation package will install a component at the root of the target file system, "Require admin authentication" is also selected.

9   Click Contents to view the list of files to be delivered together with the permissions that will be set.

> **Note** To view files and folders further down the hierarchy within the contents of this installation package, click the disclosure triangle next to each folder.

10 Click the Build icon (a hammer) in the toolbar to build your installation package.

11 Select to save your installation package ("Basic Install *n*") into your ~/Documents/Packages/ folder.

12 Click Save.

> **Warning!** During the build, PackageMaker will identify any problems you might encounter after installing this installation package on target computers. This includes (but is not limited to) any mismatched permissions modes and file or folder ownerships. Deploying an installation package that exhibits warning messages during a build may cause issues after deployment on target computers.

13 The build progress will be shown, ending in a "Build Succeeded!" message.

You have successfully created an installation package. Before you test it, you will save your PackageMaker project for use in later exercises.

14 Choose File > Save and save your PackageMaker project as "basic-*n*" in your ~/Documents/Packages folder.

Now that you've created an installation package and saved your work, it's time to test your installation package on the Client computer.

15 Close the PackageMaker window.

Test Installation Package on the Client Computer

To make sure the installation package works as expected, you will copy the installation package to your Client computer using ARD and install the installation package. Replace *n* with your student number in the following steps.

1 On your Client computer, make sure you are logged in as cadmin.

2 On your Server computer, open ARD and select your Client computer from your computer lists.

3 Click the Copy icon in the toolbar and drag your newly
   created package from ~/Documents/Packages into the
   Copy items window.

4 Select "Open items" after copying and click Copy.

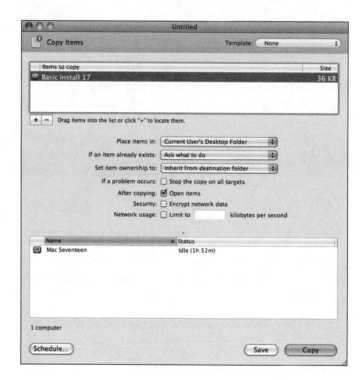

> **Note** By electing to use Copy Items (and selecting "Open
> items" after copying) the end-user will see the Installer
> application screens. When instructed to test/deploy your
> new installation packages to your Client computer, reuse
> this method utilizing ARD.

The Installer application runs on your Client computer.

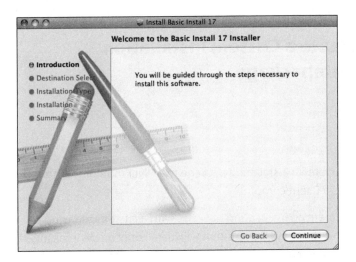

5   On your Client computer, choose Window > Installer Log and choose to show all logs from the log window that appears.

6   Follow the prompts to install the installation package onto the Client computer's boot volume; authenticate as cadmin when prompted.

7   After installation is complete, check the root level of the boot volume for a new folder called Documentation.

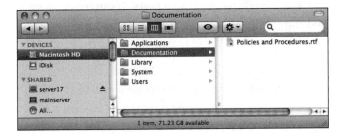

Exercise 3.1.2

Create a Custom Installation Metapackage

Objectives

- Create an installation package to deliver multiple components to a Client computer

- Create an installation package with a customized user interface and notices that will install only on systems meeting certain criteria

PackageMaker can also be used to deliver multiple installation packages containing files and folders. Installation choices can be managed so that some installation packages are required, whereas others are optional. This flexibility can be useful during deployment; for example, it allows managers to create one universal installation package that can be used on multiple computers. During installation you select only the necessary packages—thus saving time and effort. Also, PackageMaker can be used to customize the installation screens and place prerequisite conditions for the target computers where your installation packages are to be run. You will use PackageMaker to manage these choices.

In this exercise, you will add to the package you created in Exercise 3.1.1. You will add content to create a new "installation metapackage," manage installation package selections, and add additional information such as a background graphic plus license and Read Me texts. Finally, you will include criteria that will be checked during install.

Use PackageMaker to Create a Custom Installation Metapackage

Create an installation package by selecting the components in PackageMaker. Replace *n* with your student number in the following steps.

1   On your Server computer, log in as ladmin.

2   Double-click your PackageMaker project to open it
    (~/Documents/Packages/basic-*n*).

3   Choose File > Save As and save your PackageMaker document
    as "custom-*n*" within the same folder.

    This will prevent you from overwriting your basic installation
    package document.

4   Change the package title to Custom Install *n*.

5   Drag the following items from Student Materials/Chapter3 into
    the contents pane for your package:

    • Crystal Ball.app

    • TextWrangler.app

    Your installation package content lists should now show three
    components.

    Notice how the destination for the newly added components
    was set to /Applications.

6   Click the installation package icon and verify that User Sees is
    set to Easy and Custom Install.

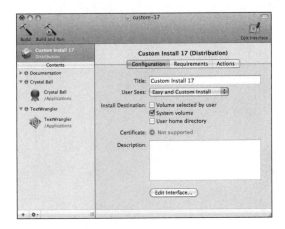

    Also, notice how the icon has changed from an Installation
    package to an Installation metapackage, and the type is now
    labeled Distribution.

The PackageMaker project file icon is slightly different from the Installation package and Installation metapackage icons:

PackageMaker project

Installation package

Installation metapackage

7   Click the first component in the Contents list (Documentation) and view the configuration information.

Be careful to click the payload title (Documentation) and not the payload contents (the Documentation folder).

By default the Choice Name is taken from the installation package item that you dragged into PackageMaker. The Identifier is generated as "choice0," "choice1," and so on as additional components are added.

8   To make sure this component is always installed, set its initial state to Selected only.

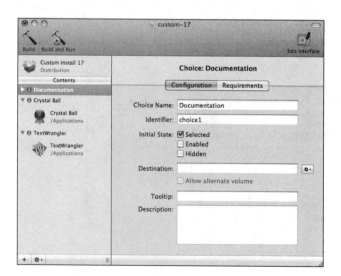

9   Save your PackageMaker project.

Next you will change the installation interface.

Use PackageMaker Interface Editor to Customize the Installation Screens

You will use PackageMaker's Interface Editor to add a background image and custom text.

1 Click Edit Interface in the toolbar (top right).

The Interface Editor opens to allow you to change the default items shown during an installation.

The background is the first item highlighted to change.

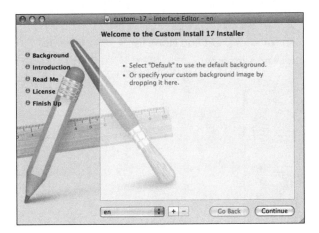

You can either drag and drop an image onto the Interface Editor to change the background, or you can select one by browsing (use the drawer on the right). You will use the browser to set the background image this time.

2 In the drawer on the right, click File for the Background and then select Choose from the Action menu.

3 Navigate to and select Student Materials/Chapter3/Resources/ PCDS-background.tiff.

4 Click Choose to add the new background image.

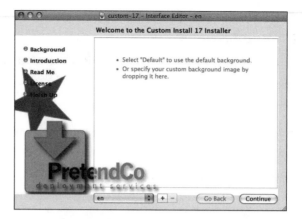

5   Select Left for Alignment and None for Scaling from the appropriate pop-up menus.

6   Click Continue to edit the Introduction screen.

7   Drag and drop the Welcome.rtf file from Student Materials/ Chapter3/Resources onto the Interface Editor.

8   Click Continue to edit the Read Me screen.

9   Use TextEdit or the Finder's QuickLook feature to view the contents of Student Material/Chapter3/Resources/ReadMe.rtf.

10 Drag and drop the ReadMe.rtf file onto the Interface Editor.

11 Click Continue to edit the License information screen.

12 Drag and drop Student Materials/Chapter3/Resources/License.rtf onto the Interface Editor to display the contents of the license text file.

13 Click Continue.

The final item in the Interface Editor is the Finish Up screen.
For now, we'll leave that screen with the default message.

14 Close the Interface Editor window.

The Interface Editor streamlines the creation of a customized
installation package. To see the installation package structure you
have built, you can view the installation package files in Raw mode.

15 Save your PackageMaker project.

16 Choose Project > Raw Editing Mode.

The PackageMaker screen will flip to show the file hierarchy of
your project.

17 Expand the Resources and en.lproj folders.

You can edit some of the text and XML files directly in Raw
editing mode—but for now, switch back to normal editing mode.

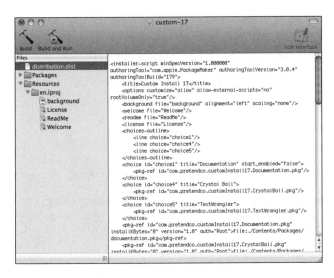

18 Choose Project > Normal Editing Mode.

19 Save your PackageMaker project.

The final step for this installation package is to add installation
requirements.

Add Installation Requirements Using PackageMaker

You will add three installation requirements for your custom installation package.

1   In PackageMaker, select your package icon once more and click the Requirements tab.

2   Click the Add button (+) to add a new requirement.

3   Leave the default If statement as Megabytes Available on Target.

4   For the condition, choose >= (greater than or equal to) and enter a value of 10240.

5   For the Failure Message, enter:

    `Insufficient disk space, 10GB is required for this install.`

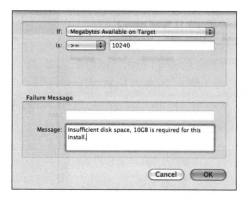

6   Click OK and then click the plus sign to add another requirement.

7   Change the condition type to If "Target OS Version (e.g. 10.x.x)."

8   Change the condition test to >= and enter a value of 10.6.1.

9   In the Failure Message area, enter:

    `Mac OS X 10.6.1 and above is required for this install.`

10 Click OK and then click the Add button (+) to add one more requirement.

11 Select If File Exists on Target.

12 Enter a file path of

`/Users/.PCDS-installOK`

13 For the Failure Message, enter:

`This package cannot be installed on non-PretendCo`
`computers.`

14 Click OK and then save your PackageMaker project.

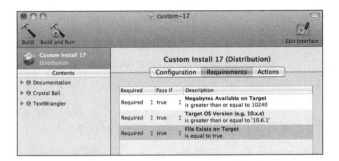

15 Click the Build icon and save your installation package as Custom-Install-*n* in your ~/Documents/Packages folder (where *n* is your student number).

> **Note** If you leave the default filename extension as .pkg, you will be prompted to change it to .mpkg for your distribution package.

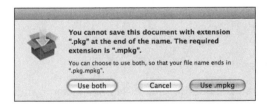

16 Click Use .mpkg and close the PackageMaker project window.

17 Click Save when prompted.

Now that you have created a custom installation metapackage with one required and two optional components, it's time to test it on your Client computer.

Test Installation Metapackage on the Client Computer

To make sure the installation package works as expected (including installation choices), you will copy the installation package to your Client computer and install the installation package using ARD.

1   On your Client computer, make sure you are logged in as cadmin.

2   On your Server computer, open ARD and select your Client computer from your computer list.

3   Click the Copy icon in the toolbar and drag your newly created custom package from ~/Documents/Packages into the Copy items window.

4   Select "Open items" after copying and click Copy.

5   On your Client computer, follow the prompts to install the installation package on to the Client computer's boot volume, authenticating when prompted.

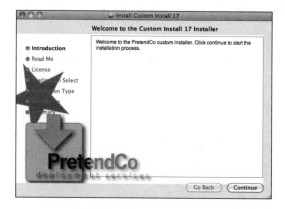

Notice the customized background, Welcome message, and License text.

Question 1   Will this installation package install successfully?

6   On your Client computer, use Terminal to issue the following command to create the file that your installation package is looking for:

`sudo touch /Users/.PCDS-installOK`

Authenticate as cadmin.

7   Run the installation package again, until the customization screen appears.

> **Note** The installer proceeds further this time because the file /Users/.PCDS-installOK now exists on the target volume.

8   Click Customize.

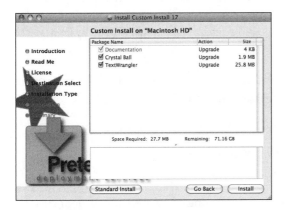

Notice that the required installation package component is grayed out but selected, indicating that you cannot deselect it.

9   Follow the prompts to install the installation package on to the client machine's boot volume, authenticating when prompted.

10 After installation is complete, the default Install Succeeded screen displays.

11 After installation is complete, check /Applications to verify that two new applications (Crystal Ball and TextWrangler) were installed.

List an Installation Package's Bill of Materials (optional)

It is often useful to find out what files were installed by a particular package. This information can be used to verify that the install proceeded as expected; it is also used by Disk Utility's Repair Permissions function.

Use `lsbom` to view the bill of materials for the package that you just installed. Replace *n* with your student number in the following steps.

1 On your Client computer, open Terminal.

2 Navigate to the Receipts folder:

`cd /var/db/receipts`

3 List the files installed by one of the packages in your custom installation using `lsbom`:

`lsbom -p UGMsF com.pretendco.custominstalln.\`
`CrystalBall.pkg.bom`

The "UGMsF" parameters specified with the "-p" option translate to:

U user (owner) name

G group name

M permissions mode

s file size

F filename in quotes

For other options, see the man page for `lsbom`.

Exercise 3.1.3
Create a Flat Installation Package

Objective

- Create an installation package that is contained within a single file (this is the default on Mac OS X v10.6)

The installation packages you have created so far include a folder structure. In some cases (such as for emailing or copying), it is beneficial to have the installation package "flattened" into a single file as opposed to placing these installation packages into a container such as a disk image. The new "flat-package" format within Mac OS X v10.6 allows you to do just that.

In this exercise you will create a new installation package within PackageMaker and then use the command line to take a look inside. You will reuse an installation package you created in Exercise 3.1.1.

1 Log in as ladmin on your Server computer.

2 Double-click the ~/Documents/Packages/basic-*n* PackageMaker project file.

3 Double-click the package icon just above the Contents pane.

   The Install Properties dialog appears.

4 Change the Minimum Target setting to Mac OS X v10.5 Leopard and click OK.

FLAT INSTALLER

5 Give your new installation package the title of "Flat Install *n*" (where *n* is your student number).

6 Choose File > Save As and save your project as flat-*n* in ~/Documents/Packages.

7 Click the Build icon in the toolbar to build your installation package.

8   Select to save your installation package as "Flat Install *n*" into
    your ~/Documents/Packages/ folder.

9   Click Save.

10 Close the PackageMaker window and click Save when prompted.

11 Open Terminal and perform a long listing of ~/Documents/
    Packages:

    `ls -l ~/Documents/Packages/`

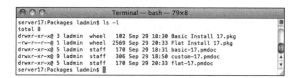

Note that all your earlier installation packages and the
PackageMaker projects are folders except for the Flat Install *n*.pkg.

There are a few useful commands you can use to examine flat
installation packages.

12 Examine the installation package contents / BOM:

    `pkgutil --payload-files ~/Documents/Packages/\`
    `Flat\ Install\ n.pkg`

13 Expand the contents of the installation package with this com-
    mand, all on one line:

    `pkgutil --expand ~/Documents/Packages/Flat\ \`
    `Install\ n.pkg ~/Documents/Packages/flatn`

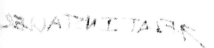

Take a look in the newly created flat*n* folder at the files that
have been extracted.

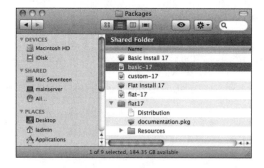

Installation Package Features and Deployment

3.2

In this lesson you'll dig deeper into the installation package technology and explore some of the advanced features that allow you to deploy automated tasks, scripts, and even repackaged contents from other installations. You will also learn how to effectively deploy installation packages, including using ARD to quickly distribute installation packages to multiple computers simultaneously. Finally, you will learn how to monitor and repair items after they have been installed.

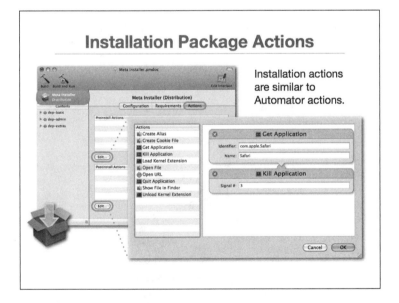

For details, see "Using Installation Action Workflows" in Chapter 3 of *Apple Training Series: Mac OS X Deployment v10.6*.

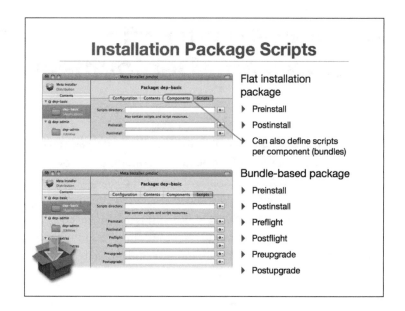

For details, see "Using Scripts in Installation Packages" in Chapter 3 of *Apple Training Series: Mac OS X Deployment v10.6*.

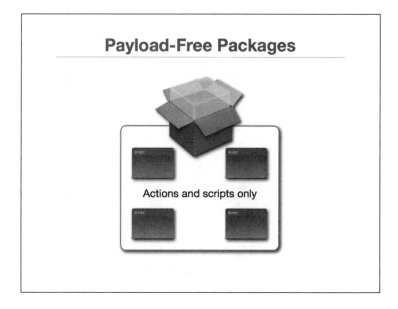

For details, see "Using Scripts in Installation Packages" in Chapter 3 of *Apple Training Series: Mac OS X Deployment v10.6*.

For details, see "Creating Snapshot Installation Packages" in
Chapter 3 of *Apple Training Series: Mac OS X Deployment v10.6.*

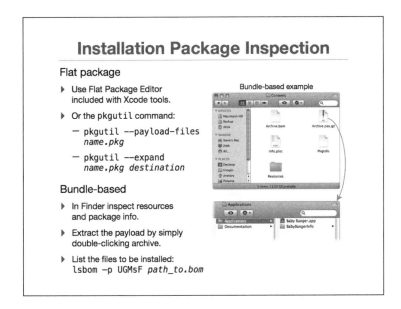

For details, see "Inspecting Installation Packages" in Chapter 3 of
Apple Training Series: Mac OS X Deployment v10.6.

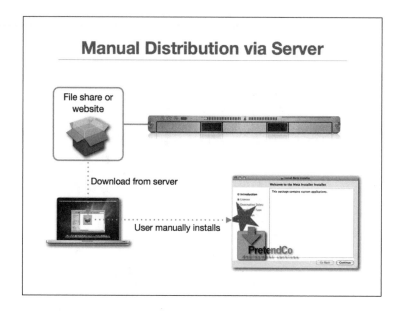

For details, see "Deploying Installation Packages" in Chapter 3 of
Apple Training Series: Mac OS X Deployment v10.6.

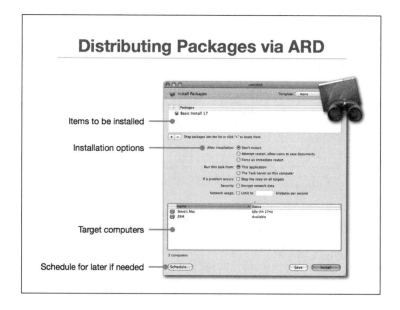

For details, see "Deploying Installation Packages" in Chapter 3 of
Apple Training Series: Mac OS X Deployment v10.6.

Distributing Packages via SSH

`tar —cvf ./Basic.tgz ./Basic\ Install\ N.pkg`

▶ Archive (bundle-based only)

`scp ./Basic.tgz cadmin@client—number.local:/tmp`

▶ Securely copy installer file to client

`ssh cadmin@client—number.local`

▶ Remote login to client and control it

`tar —xvf /tmp/Basic.tgz`

▶ Unarchive (bundle-based only)

`sudo installer —pkg Basic\ Install\ N.pkg —target /`

▶ Install package

For details, see "Deploying Installation Packages" in Chapter 3 of *Apple Training Series: Mac OS X Deployment v10.6.*

Installation History

Legacy receipt database (/Library/Receipts) may contain "old-style" receipts if system was upgraded or migrated.

Mac OS X v10.6 now maintains list of updates after system installation in /Library/Receipts/InstallHistory.plist.

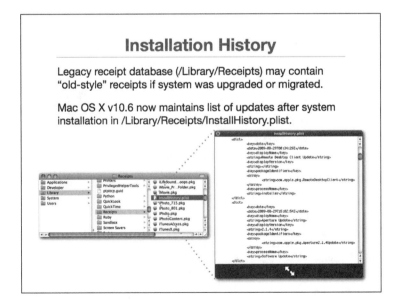

For details, see "Installation Package Maintenance" in Chapter 3 of *Apple Training Series: Mac OS X Deployment v10.6.*

Installation Receipt Database

The receipts database tracks information about all installed packages, including payload items and permissions.

Mac OS X v10.6 receipt database stored in /var/db/receipts, in this folder each previously installed item will have two files:

▶ A .plist file containing general information about the install

▶ A .bom file containing the payload list and permissions

For details, see "Installation Package Maintenance" in Chapter 3 of *Apple Training Series: Mac OS X Deployment v10.6.*

Installation Maintenance

Verify proper installation

▶ Use Console application to view /private/var/log/install.log.

▶ Repair permissions (details in next slide).

Gather information from receipt database

▶ List installed package IDs: pkgutil --pkgs

▶ General information: pkgutil --pkg-info *packageid*

▶ List installation payload: pkgutil --files *packageid*

▶ List installation payload with ownership and permissions:
lsbom -p UGMsF /var/db/receipts/*packageid*.bom

Reinstall an installation package

▶ If receipt is present, the Installer will perform an upgrade install, which often will not not replace any possibly corrupted items.

▶ Remove receipt from the database to fully reinstall:
sudo pkgutil --forget *packageid*.

For details, see "Installation Package Maintenance" in Chapter 3 of *Apple Training Series: Mac OS X Deployment v10.6.*

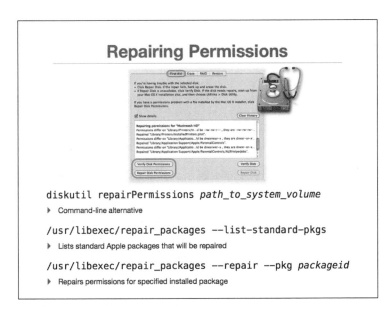

For details, see "Installation Package Maintenance" in Chapter 3 of
Apple Training Series: Mac OS X Deployment v10.6.

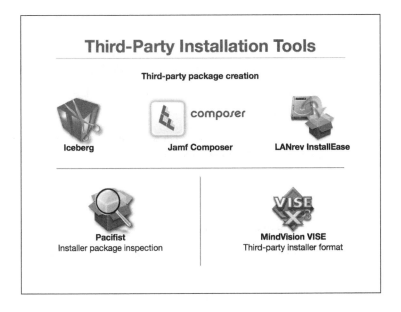

For details, see "Third-Party Installation Tools" in Chapter 3 of
Apple Training Series: Mac OS X Deployment v10.6.

Exercise 3.2.1

Create an Installation Package with Scripts

Objective

- Create an installation package that delivers a payload and executes scripts/actions on the target computer

You can create scripts that, when added to an installation package, allow you to control certain aspects of the installation. An example might be to check for the presence of other software or maybe to perform specific pre- or postinstallation tasks.

In this exercise you will edit the custom installation package that you created in Exercise 3.1.3 to add in a preinstall script and a postinstall action. Replace n with your student number in the following steps.

Create a New Installation Package with a Preinstall Script and Postinstall Action

Create an installation package that will rename a file if it exists on the target install volume.

1   On your Server computer, double-click the flat-n PackageMaker project located in ~/Documents/Packages.

2   Choose File > Save As.

3   Name the new copy of this document custom2-n and save it within the same folder (~/Documents/Packages).

4   Within PackageMaker, change the title of this installation package to "Custom S+A Install n."

5   Expand the contents for this installation package and then click its folder (Documentation) and click Scripts.

6   For the preinstall script entry, choose Student Materials/ Chapter3/roll-policy-doc.

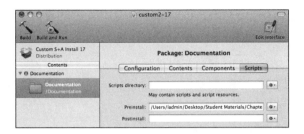

To see what the script does, open it with TextWrangler or
QuickLook.

> **Note** Prior to Mac OS X v10.5, preinstall scripts had to be
> called "preinstall" (likewise for postinstall and so on). In
> Mac OS X v10.6, you can use any file for the standard scripts,
> and PackageMaker will automatically rename them for you.

The next step is to add a postinstall action.

Add a Postinstall Action to Open the Policies and Procedures Document

You will add in a postinstall action in much the same way that you
can edit workflows with Automator.

1   In PackageMaker, select your installation package on the left,
    instead of the installation component to which you were previ-
    ously adding a script, and click Actions.

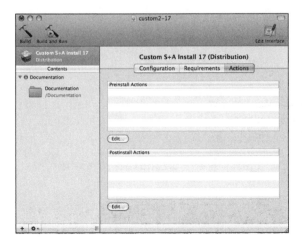

2 Click Edit under the Postinstall Actions window.

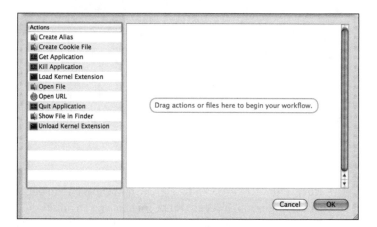

3 Drag the Open File action into the workflow window.

4 Change the type to Absolute Path and enter /Documentation/ Policies and Procedures.rtf into the filename.

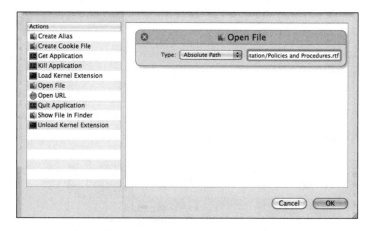

5 Click OK and then click Build.

6 Save your installation package as CustomS+A Install *n* in ~/Documents/Packages.

7 Close the PackageMaker window and click Save when prompted.

8   Test this installation package on your Client computer.

You should end up with a new copy of Policies and Procedures.
rtf that automatically opens after the install, plus an additional
time-stamped Policies and Procedures document.

Exercise 3.2.2

Create a Payload-Free Installation Package

Objective

- Create an installation package that executes scripts only on a target computer

Not only can installation packages contain scripts (which allow you to control certain aspects of the installation) in some situations, but that's all your installation package might contain. An installation package that has scripts and that copies no files to the target computer is said to be payload-free.

An example might be an installation package that is created to fix a known problem or alter the configuration on all computers department-wide. In this exercise you will create a payload-free installation package to install a new administrator account on your Client computer. Later on you'll learn how to hide this new account.

Create a New Installation Package to Add the Hidden Administrator Account

Create an installation package that will create a new user account on the install volume.

1   On your Server computer, open PackageMaker (or click its icon in the Dock) and verify that the Minimum Target is set to Mac OS X v10.5.

    Because some of the commands used when creating the new administrator will work only in Mac OS X v10.5 and above, you'll also need to add a Requirement to your installation package.

2   Set the title of the installation package to be Install Administrator Account.

3   Set the Install Destination to be the "System volume" only.

4   Click Requirements.

5   Add a condition to allow installs only on target computers
    with Mac OS X v10.5 and above and set the failure message to
    the following:

    `This installer needs 10.5 or above.`

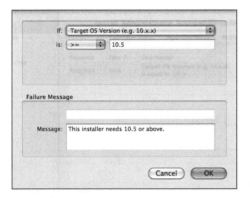

6   Click OK.

7   For your new installation package, drag the folder Student
    Materials/Chapter3/Payload-Free (an empty folder) into the
    contents window.

8   Deselect Enabled for the newly added component title.

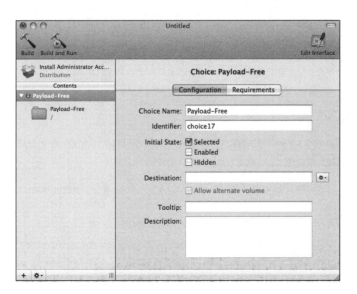

By deselecting the Enabled option, you remove the user's ability to deselect part of the installation package. In other words, the script that runs with this component will be required.

9   Select the newly added component folder (the Payload-Free folder) and click Contents.

> **Note** Scripts such as Postinstall are associated with an installation package component. Even though this is a payload-free installation package, you still need to add the component first.

10 Deselect the Payload-Free entry.

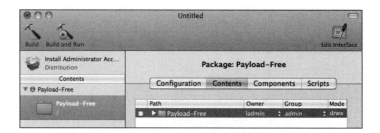

There will be no files to copy with this installation package—just script execution.

11 Click the Scripts tab and set the Postinstall script to Student Materials/Chapter3/ install-admin.

12 Save your project as Hadmin-*n* (where *n* is your student number) in ~/Documents/Packages.

13 Click Build.

14 Save your installation package as Install Hadmin *n*.pkg in the same folder (where *n* is your student number).

15 Close the PackageMaker window and click Save when prompted.

Test the Customized Installation Package

You will copy the installation package to your Client computer and install the installation package using ARD.

1   On your Client computer, make sure you are logged in as cadmin.

2   On your Server computer, open ARD and select your Client computer from your computer list.

3   Click the Copy icon in the toolbar and drag your newly created custom package from ~/Documents/Packages into the "Copy items" window.

4   Select "Open items" after copying and click Copy.

5   On your Client computer, follow the prompts to install the installation package on to the Client computer's boot volume, authenticating when prompted.

> **Note** The Continue button will be unavailable until you click "Install for all users of this machine."

6   After installation is complete, open System Preferences.

7   Click Accounts and change the Login Options to show the Login window as Name and Password (authenticate as hadmin, password "secrets").

    You should be able to use the new administrator account for authenticating system-wide changes like this.

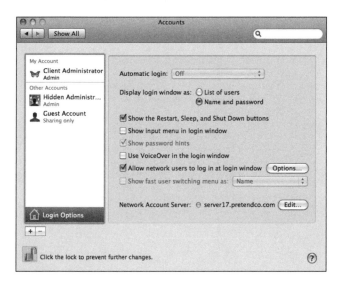

8   Log out of the Client computer and then log in as user hadmin (password "secrets").

9   When prompted for managed preference usage, click "remember my choice" and click Disable.

Once logged in, you should see hadmin's desktop with hadmin's home folder shown in the sidebar as .hadmin.

10 Log out and then log back in again as cadmin.

Again, disable managed client preference usage for this administrator account.

11 On your Server computer, open Remote Desktop and try to control the Client computer.

Question 2 Were you able to control the computer?

12 Edit the entry in computer list lab1 so that the hadmin account is used to contact the Client computer.

13 Try to control that computer again.

Question 3 Were you successful?

Exercise 3.2.3
Create a Snapshot Installation Package

Objective

- Create a standard installation package from a third-party installer package

When you deploy complex systems, using a uniform set of tools reduces the risks of software incompatibilities and mistakes. For example, some third-party applications use VISE for installation, which does not generate an installation package receipt.

In this exercise you will identify where the components of an application get installed by a non-Apple installation utility and repackage those components into a custom installation package.

Normally you would install software onto a Client computer and use PackageMaker on that computer to create a snapshot installation package. To save time and to avoid installing Xcode on the Client computer, you will run the software install on your Server.

Create a Snapshot Installation Package

You will start with PackageMaker.

1   Open PackageMaker (or click its icon in the Dock) and accept the defaults for your new installation package.

2   Choose Project > Add Snapshot Package.

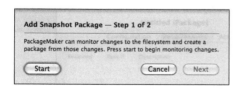

3   Click Start.

Install Software Without Using the Apple Installer

You will install AppleWorks and capture this event using PackageMaker.

1 Double-click the package file named AppleWorks Install – US and Canada that's located in the folder Student Materials/ Chapter3/.

2 Follow the steps to install AppleWorks on your Server's volume.

3 Click Quit when the installation has completed.

Complete the Snapshot Installation Package

Now you will add the installed components to your PackageMaker project.

1 Back in PackageMaker, click Stop and then click Next to add the components to the project.

2 Uncheck all the files except for AppleWorks 6.

If you were creating your own Snapshot installation package, you would review all the folders listed in the Snapshot Package window and include all necessary application and application support files.

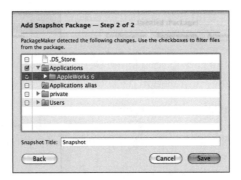

In this case, we are just interested in AppleWorks 6, which was installed in the Applications folder.

3 Change the Snapshot Title to AppleWorks 6 and click Save.

4 Change the title of the installation package to "Install AW6 Standard *n*" (where *n* is your student number).

5 Change the install destination to use the System volume only.

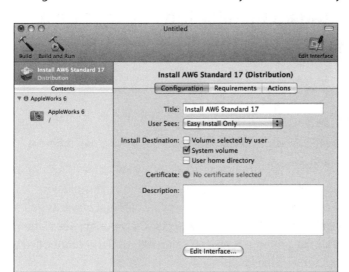

6 Save your document as "AW6 Std *n*" in ~/Documents/Packages.

7 Click Build and save your installation package as
AppleWorks6-*n*.pkg.

8 If you receive any warnings during the build process, apply the
recommendations and try the build again (replacing your built
installation package).

9 Close the PackageMaker window and click Save when prompted.

10 Test this installation package on your Client computer.

AppleWorks 6 requires that Rosetta be installed on your client
computer—therefore you may also see the Software Update
application attempt to install Rosetta if Rosetta was not
included in your Client computer's initial software install.

> **Note** Multiple snapshot installation packages may be
> combined into one installation metapackage depending
> on how many different installation packages you need to
> run. Snapshots can also capture file system changes from
> drag-and-drop installs into the Applications folder.

Install an Installation Package on a Remote Computer

Objective

- Install packages on remote computers using two different methods

You can execute the delivery and installation of installation packages to remote computers in a few different ways. As you saw in Exercise 2.1.2, you copied a Mac OS X Update installation package to a remote computer using ARD and then controlled that computer to install the update.

In the following exercise you will use two more techniques for installing installation packages on remote computers: the command line and ARD (without controlling a screen).

Enable Remote Login on Client Computer

To be able to send and install the installation package remotely, Remote Login needs to be turned on for your Client computer.

1 On your client machine, open System Preferences and click Sharing.

2 Select Remote Login and leave all other defaults.

   Remote users can now log in to the client machine using the encrypted SSH protocol to access the command line and securely copy files.

Remotely Install a Installation Package Using the Command Line

You will copy an installation package, one you have used previously, from your Server computer to your Client computer with scp and then you will install the installation package.

1 Open Terminal on your server and navigate to your ~/Documents/Packages folder with the following command:

```
cd ~/Documents/Packages
```

2 Next, create an archive of the installation package you created in Exercise 3.1.1 (Basic Install *n*.pkg) and then securely copy the archive to the /tmp folder on your Client computer:

```
tar -cvf Basic.tar Basic\ Install\ n.pkg
```

```
scp Basic.tar cadmin@Mac-Number.local:/tmp
```

Replace *n* with your student number and replace *Number* with your student number spelled out (for example, *17* would be *Seventeen*).

If this is your first time connecting to a computer using SSH, you will be prompted to continue the connection (type yes) and then provide the password for user cadmin.

3 Remotely log in to the Client computer:

```
ssh cadmin@Mac-Number.local
```

Again, provide cadmin's password.

4 Unarchive and use the installer command-line tool to install the installation package:

```
cd /tmp
```

```
sudo tar -xvf Basic.tar
```

Again, provide cadmin's password.

```
sudo installer -pkg Basic\ Install\ n.pkg \-target /
```

5 Authenticate with cadmin's password (if necessary) to complete the install.

The installer command will report its progress during the install:

```
Mac-Seventeen:tmp cadmin$ sudo installer -pkg Basic\ Install\ 17.pkg -target /
installer: Package name is Basic Install 17
installer: Upgrading at base path /
2009-09-29 21:31:57.011 installer[1880:742b] using receipt prefix of Documentation
installer: The upgrade was successful.
Mac-Seventeen:tmp cadmin$
```

> **Note** If you were installing this package for the first time, the installer would report a successful install as opposed to a successful upgrade.

6   Type exit to close the connection to your Client computer.

   You have now successfully copied and installed an installation package using only the command line.

Remotely Install an Installation Package Using ARD

This time you will use ARD's Install Packages feature to deploy an installation package from your server to your Client computer.

1   On your Server computer, open Remote Desktop and select the lab1 computer list.

2   Select your Client computer from the list and choose Manage > Install Packages.

3   Click the plus sign under the installation package list window and select the same Basic Install *n*.pkg you used during the previous command-line install method.

4   Start the installation by clicking Install.

   ARD will report the progress of both the installation package copy and installation.

You have now successfully installed an installation package remotely using ARD's Install Package feature.

> **Note** Installations can be executed on multiple computers
> at the same time using ARD, whereas you have to log in
> to one computer at a time using the ssh and installer
> commands. However, with ARD's "Send UNIX command"
> feature, you can issue UNIX commands to multiple comput-
> ers at the same time.

Update Your Deployment Planning Template

In the previous exercises you have created a variety of installation packages using PackageMaker. Installation packages are particularly useful for encapsulating software updates, files, and applications for delivery locally or across the Internet to Client computers with pinpoint accuracy.

Now it's time to update your template to see which of the various methods demonstrated lend themselves to your particular situation:

- Using basic installation packages

- Using installation metapackages

- Using installation package scripts (including payload-free)

- Using snapshot installation packages

When filling out your template, please remember to include the rationale for using these forms of deployment.

4

Creating
System Images

4.1   System Customization and Cloned
          System Images

Exercise 4.1.1   Customize Client Settings

Exercise 4.1.2   Create a System Image from a Client

4.2   System Image Utility (SIU) and
          Modular System Images

Exercise 4.2.1   Build a Modular NetRestore Image Using SIU

Exercise 4.2.2   Create a Cloned NetRestore Image Using SIU
          (optional)

Exercise 4.2.3   Update Your Deployment Planning Template

4.1

System Customization and Cloned System Images

The ability to deploy an entire operating system quickly and consistently is the centerpiece of most deployment solutions. Indeed, the act of imaging, or restoring, an entire operating system to deployed computers is the easiest way to ensure that all your systems are similar. In most situations maintaining a consistent system across all your deployed computers leads to the best experience for both users and administrators alike.

Before you create a system image, however, you must prepare the custom configurations that will be part of your image. One of the primary advantages to using system images is, after all, the ability to deploy a majority of the system configuration along with the system software. The first part of this lesson focuses on techniques for customizing and configuring a deployed system. Specifically, this lesson will cover advanced techniques that go beyond what is available with the standard graphical administration tools. This also includes advanced Mac OS X client management configuration.

Ultimately, in this chapter you will create multiple Mac OS X system images, optimized for deployment, using two different techniques. The first technique covered in this lesson, creating a cloned system image, is the classic method that's easier to implement but has some baggage. The second technique, creating a modular system image, you will meet in the next lesson.

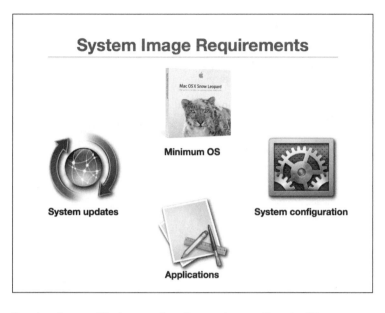

For details, see "Understanding System Image Creation" in Chapter 4 of *Apple Training Series: Mac OS X Deployment v10.6.*

Customizing Deployed Systems

System customization provides several advantages:

▸ Simplify the user experience.

▸ Prevent system modification or improper use.

▸ Present company or institutional branding and usage policies.

▸ Provide helpful information to the user.

Three general implementation methods:

▸ Ideally managed via directory services–based managed preferences, also known as MCX

▸ Settings that are configured as part of your system image

▸ Settings that are applied via scripting and automation as a postimaging task on each client

PretendCo
deployment services

For details, see "Understanding System Image Creation" in Chapter 4 of *Apple Training Series: Mac OS X Deployment v10.6.*

Overview of Managed Preferences

System to provide centralized managed configuration

Configuration lies within some form of directory services:

▶ Local directory node

▶ Open Directory master

▶ Properly configured third-party directory

Management available at several levels, are merged at login:

▶ Workgroup

▶ Computer group

▶ Computer

▶ User

For details, see "Integrating with Managed Preferences" in Chapter 4 of *Apple Training Series: Mac OS X Deployment v10.6*.

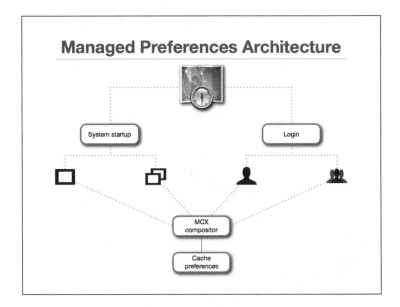

For details, see "Integrating with Managed Preferences" in Chapter 4 of *Apple Training Series: Mac OS X Deployment v10.6*.

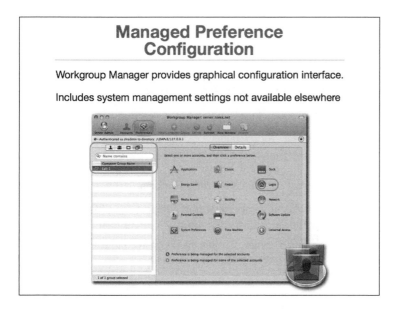

For details, see "Integrating with Managed Preferences" in
Chapter 4 of *Apple Training Series: Mac OS X Deployment v10.6.*

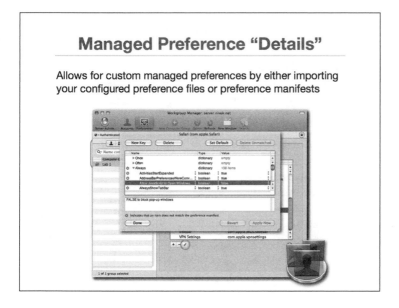

For details, see "Integrating with Managed Preferences" in
Chapter 4 of *Apple Training Series: Mac OS X Deployment v10.6.*

Preference Manifests

Files embedded in the application bundle that describe an application's preferences

Import using Details pane of Workgroup Manager

▸ Select the specific preference file.

▸ Select the application bundle (icon).

▸ Select /System/Library/CoreServices/ManagedClient.app for various system preference manifests.

Few third-party applications support manifests, but you can attempt to manage with "often"

▸ The "often" behavior writes the configured preference file to the home folder every time the user logs in.

For details, see "Integrating with Managed Preferences" in Chapter 4 of *Apple Training Series: Mac OS X Deployment v10.6.*

Troubleshooting Managed Preferences

Determine managed preferences results

▸ System Profiler > Software > Managed Client

▸ mcxquery –user *username*

Preference cache locations

▸ Local Directory

▸ /Library/Managed Preferences

▸ ~/Library/Preferences

▸ ~/.account

▸ /var/db/.AccessibilityAPIEnabled

mcxrefresh –u *username*

▸ Forces the client to reevaluate management for user

For details, see "Integrating with Managed Preferences" in Chapter 4 of *Apple Training Series: Mac OS X Deployment v10.6.*

User Home Folder Template

New user home folders are created based on content of /System/Library/User Template/English.lproj/ folder.

Customize to fit your deployment needs, but you must have root (sudo) access to modify contents.

Upon user home creation, ownership is transferred to the new user account; use special permissions to lock items:

▸ sudo chown root:wheel *path*

▸ sudo chmod 664 *path*

▸ sudo chflags uchg *path*

For details, see "Customize System Configuration" in Chapter 4 of *Apple Training Series: Mac OS X Deployment v10.6.*

Modify Setup Assistant

/System/Library/CoreServices/Setup Assistant.app/Contents /Resources/TransitionSection.bundle/Contents/Resources/

▸ intro.mov

▸ intro-sound.mp3

Force Setup Assistant to run at next startup:

▸ sudo rm /var/db/.AppleSetupDone

For details, see "Customize System Configuration" in Chapter 4 of *Apple Training Series: Mac OS X Deployment v10.6.*

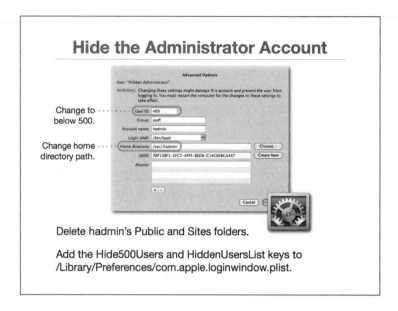

For details, see "Customize System Configuration" in Chapter 4 of *Apple Training Series: Mac OS X Deployment v10.6.*

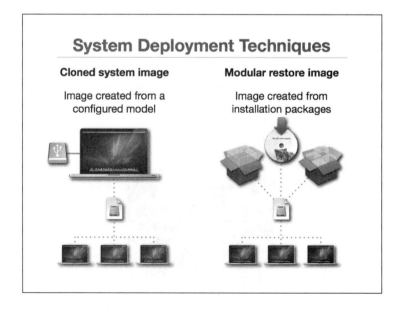

For details, see "Understanding System Image Creation" in Chapter 4 of *Apple Training Series: Mac OS X Deployment v10.6.*

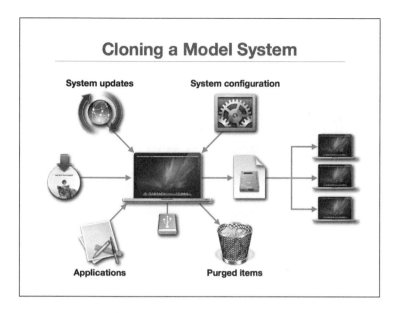

For details, see "Cloned Image: Overview and Preparation" in Chapter 4 of *Apple Training Series: Mac OS X Deployment v10.6.*

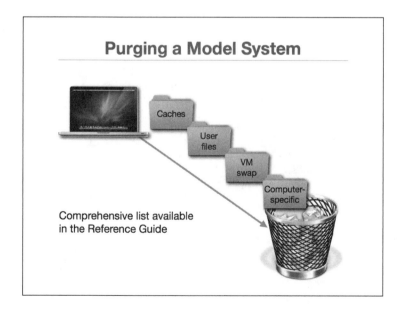

For details, see "Cloned Image: Clean Up System" in Chapter 4 of *Apple Training Series: Mac OS X Deployment v10.6.*

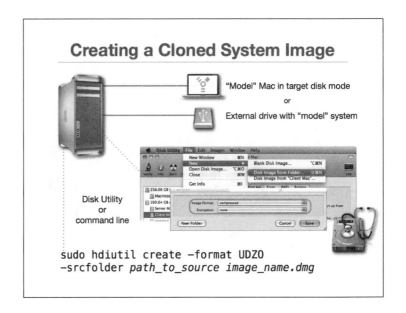

For details, see "Cloned Image: Create Restore Image" in Chapter 4 of *Apple Training Series: Mac OS X Deployment v10.6.*

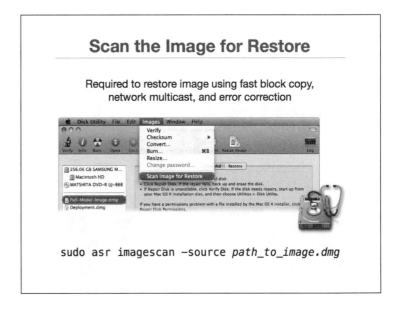

For details, see "Cloned Image: Create Restore Image" in Chapter 4 of *Apple Training Series: Mac OS X Deployment v10.6.*

Exercise 4.1.1
Customize Client Settings

Objectives

- Customize the Client computer with managed preference settings

- Customize the Client computer with local system customizations

- Clean up the Client computer for imaging

To customize your client machine and to prevent unnecessary computer-specific files from being included in your deployment system image, you will need to perform a few preparatory tasks.

Preparing a client machine involves enforcing managed preference settings from a Directory Server, customizing local system settings to supplement those that are centrally managed, removing cache files, installing necessary updates, and testing certain applications according to your organization's policies.

As a part of this exercise, you will prepare your Client computer for use with Disk Utility. Your Client computer, already bound to your Open Directory server, will be used as the source for image creation.

Set Managed Preference Settings with Workgroup Manager

You will set a new desktop background and custom login window settings using Workgroup Manager. First, set the new background picture and set login window preferences with Workgroup Manager.

1   Log in to your server as ladmin and copy PCDS-background.jpg from the Student Materials/Chapter4 folder to /Library/Desktop Pictures on the Server computer.

2   On your Server computer, open System Preferences and set your desktop picture to the new image you just copied (PCDS-background.jpg).

159

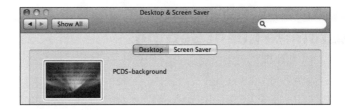

3   Close System Preferences, open Workgroup Manager, and authenticate as diradmin.

You will use your server's desktop preference file as a manifest preference to be sent to your Client computer.

4   Click the computer groups button and select your computer group Lab 1.

5   Click the Preferences icon in the toolbar.

6   Click the details button on the Preferences window.

7   Click the Add (+) button to add a new preference manifest.

8   Navigate to and select ~/Library/Preferences/com.apple.desktop.plist and select Always from the pop-up menu.

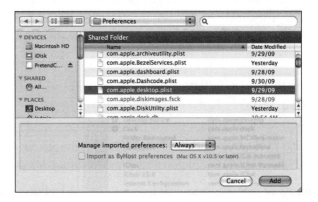

9   Click Add.

10 Select the newly added preference and click Edit (pencil) to see the new settings.

11 Remove the "numbered" dictionary key directly below the Background dictionary key and click Apply Now.

This corresponds to computer-specific information not necessary for our preference manifest.

12 Click Done.

In order for this preference manifest to work, you will need to copy the customized desktop picture to the Client computer. You will do that now.

1 Open Remote Desktop and select your Client computer from the Lab 1 list.

2 Choose Manage > Copy Items.

3 Drag the PCDS-background.jpg file from the Student Materials/Chapter4 folder into the Copy Items window.

4 Change "Place items in" to "Specify full path," type /Library/Desktop Pictures, click OK, and then click Copy.

5 Next, use the Send UNIX command, as root, to send your Client computer the following three commands:

```
chmod ug=rw,o=r /Library/Desktop\ Pictures/\
PCDS-background.jpg
```

```
chown root:admin /Library/Desktop\ Pictures/\
PCDS-background.jpg
```

```
chflags uchg /Library/Desktop\ Pictures/\
PCDS-background.jpg
```

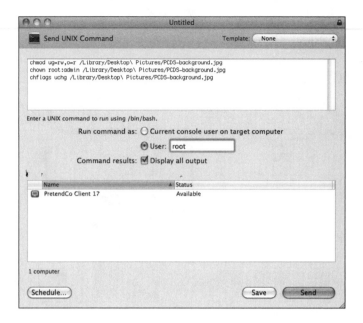

6   Click Send.

Next you will set more managed preferences for the login window.

1   In Workgroup Manager on your server, select your computer group Lab 1.

2   Click the Preferences icon in the toolbar and click the Overview button.

3   Click the Login icon and then click the Window button and set the management choice to Always.

4   Change the heading to Directory Status and enter the following text for Message:

    You are the key to PretendCo's security. By logging in to this computer you agree to abide by the terms and conditions set forth in our computer-usage policies and procedures.

5   Change the style to "Name and password text fields."

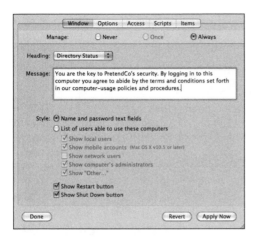

6   Click the Options button (which is already managed) and disable automatic login.

7   Enable Fast User Switching and enable user log out after 40 minutes of inactivity.

8   Leave all other settings.

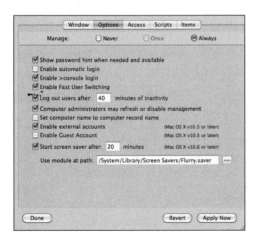

9   Click Apply Now and then click Done.

10 Click the System Preferences icon and set the management choice to Always.

11 Deselect the desktop and Screen Saver.

12 Click Apply Now and then click Done.

13 Log out of your Client computer and back in as cadmin (allow-
ing managed preferences) to confirm that the new preferences
have taken effect:

- New customized login window

- All user accounts receive the custom desktop picture

No change allowed for the desktop picture

Set Local Customizations

To further customize the user's "out-of-the-box" experience, you
will now replace the startup movie with one of PretendCo's (first
making a backup of the existing files):

1 On your server, open Remote Desktop and select your Client
computer from the lab1 list.

2 Choose Manage > Copy Items.

3 Drag the startup-stuff folder from the Student Materials/
Chapter4 folder into the Copy Items window.

4 Change "Place items in" to "Specify full path," type
/Users/Shared, and then click Copy.

5 Next, use these Terminal commands on your Client computer to
place the media files in the correct location:

```
cd /System/Library/CoreServices/Setup\ \
Assistant.app/Contents/Resources/\
TransitionSection.bundle/Contents/Resources

sudo mv intro.mov intro.mov.old

sudo mv intro-sound.mp3 intro-sound.mp3.old

sudo cp /Users/Shared/startup-stuff/intro.mov .

sudo cp /Users/Shared/startup-stuff/intro-sound.mp3 .
```

6 Close your Terminal window and log out of your Client computer.

You have now applied preferences for the Login window, the
desktop picture, and the startup movie.

Hide the Hidden Administrator Account

You will customize the hadmin account's Dock and then hide the account from all other users of the computer.

1 On your Client computer, log in as hadmin (password: secrets).

2 Change the Dock items for hadmin to contain *only* the following:

- Finder, Dashboard, Safari, Time Machine, and System Preferences

- Airport Utility, Console, Disk Utility, Network Utility, and Terminal

- Ticket Viewer, Network Diagnostic, Screen Sharing, and Software Update (these applications are available from /System/Library/CoreServices)

- Downloads Folder and Trash

Remember, ARD has been configured for this account. If you did not test remotely controlling your Client computer with the hadmin credentials, do so now from your Server computer.

The next step is to hide the Hidden Administrator account.

3 Log out of hadmin's account and log back in as cadmin.

4 In System Preferences click Accounts (authenticate as cadmin as necessary).

5 Right-click the hadmin account to access Advanced Options.

6 Change the User ID for hadmin to 499 and click OK.

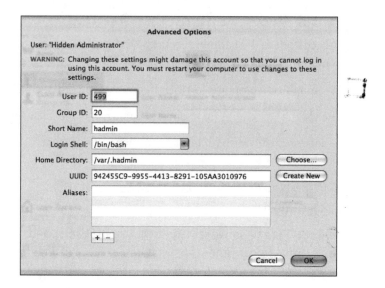

7 Open Terminal and update the ownership of hadmin's home folder to reflect the UID change:

```
sudo chown -R hadmin /var/.hadmin
```

8 Within hadmin's home folder, remove two of the default shared folders:

```
sudo rm -r /var/.hadmin/Public /var/.hadmin/Sites
```

9 Next, change the login window, fast user switching, and System Preferences to not show the hadmin account:

```
sudo defaults write /Library/Preferences/com.\
apple.loginwindow Hide500Users -bool TRUE
```

```
sudo defaults write /Library/Preferences/com.\
apple.loginwindow HiddenUsersList -array hadmin
```

10 Log out and then log back in as cadmin.

Question 1 Is the hadmin account visible in System Preferences Accounts or in the Fast User Switching menu?

Clean Up the cadmin User Account

1   Log out and log back in as hadmin.

2   Open System Preferences and click Accounts.

3   Authenticate as hadmin.

4   In the Accounts preference, remove the cadmin user, or any
    other users (except for hadmin and guest), making sure to
    delete any home folders.

> **Note** The following commands can be used to sanitize a
> user's home folder without deleting the user.
>
> ```
> rm ~/Send\ Registration
> ```
> ```
> rm -rf ~/Downloads/*
> ```
> ```
> rm -rf ~/Library/Caches/*
> ```
> ```
> rm -rf ~/Library/Preferences/ByHost/*
> ```

Your Client computer is nearly ready for imaging. For now, you
have cleaned as much as possible on a booted volume. You
will be able to complete additional cleanup once your Client
computer is connected to your Server computer.

Exercise 4.1.2

Create a System Image from a Client

Objective

- Use Disk Utility to clone the OS install from a model machine (booted into target disk mode) connected to your workstation with a FireWire cable

Disk Utility is the primary tool for creating images of systems that can be delivered locally (that is, with computers directly connected with FireWire or USB cables) or across the network (using asr in combination with NetBoot services).

In this exercise you will use Disk Utility to create a system image of your Client computer and then prepare it for deployment back to the same computer.

Before you can image the Client computer you will place it in target disk mode and complete a few additional cleanup steps.

Place Client Computer in Target Disk Mode and Connect to Server Computer

To image your Client computer using Disk Utility, you will connect it to your Server computer with a FireWire cable.

1   On your Client computer, open System Preferences.

2   From the Startup Disk pane, click Target Disk Mode and click Restart (authenticate if necessary).

    Your Client computer will now restart in target disk mode.

3   Connect your Client computer to your Server computer with a FireWire cable (available from your instructor).

    Your Client computer is now ready to be imaged.

4   On your Server computer, if prompted, cancel the Time Machine dialog.

You do not want to use your Client computer's hard drive as a Time Machine repository.

5   In the Finder, click the Client computer's hard drive name on the desktop and change it to PretendcoSystem.

This will help avoid confusion if both your Server and Client computer's hard drives are named Macintosh HD.

6   Open Terminal and complete the Client computer cleanup. First, get a root shell by executing the command:

```
sudo -s
```

Then, execute the following commands:

```
rm /Volumes/PretendcoSystem/Documentation/old_*
```

```
rm -rf /Volumes/PretendcoSystem/Users/Shared/*
```

```
rm -rf /Volumes/PretendcoSystem/Library/Caches/*
```

```
rm -rf /Volumes/PretendcoSystem/System/Library/Caches/*
```

```
rm -rf /Volumes/PretendcoSystem/private/var/db/krb5kdc
```

```
rm -f /Volumes/PretendcoSystem/private/etc/ssh_host*
```

```
rm -rf /Volumes/PretendcoSystem/private/var/db/volinfo.
database
```

```
rm -rf /Volumes/PretendcoSystem/private/var/vm/swap*
```

```
rm -rf /Volumes/PretendcoSystem/private/var/vm/sleepimage
```

```
rm -f /Volumes/PretendcoSystem/private/var/db/.
configureLocalKDC
```

```
rm -f /Volumes/PretendcoSystem/private/var/db/.
AppleSetupDone
```

```
rm -f /Volumes/PretendcoSystem/private/var/db/SystemKey
```

```
rm -f /Volumes/PretendcoSystem/Library/Keychains/System.
keychain
```

```
rm -rf /Volumes/PretendcoSystem/Library/Managed\
Preferences
```

You are now ready for imaging.

Use Disk Utility to Create a System Image

1 On your Server computer, open Disk Utility.

2 Choose File > New > Disk Image from Folder.

3 Select your Client computer's system volume
(PretendcoSystem) from the list under DEVICES and click Image.

4 Save your image as full-image-*n*.dmg into ~/Documents/Images.

5 Choose read-only for the Image Format.

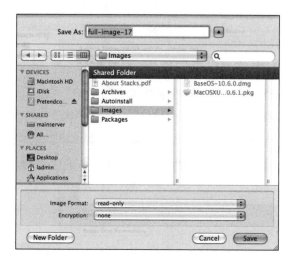

Read-only images take up more space than compressed
images, but take less time to create (and in some situations
need less time to deploy).

6 Click Save.

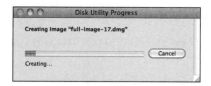

The imaging process will take approximately 10 to 40 minutes,
depending on the speed of the classroom computers.

Once the image has been created, it will show up in Disk
Utility's source list.

7 Select your new image in the source list and choose Images >
   Scan Image for Restore.

8 Authenticate as ladmin once more.

   The scanning process will take approximately 10 to 40 minutes,
   depending on the speed of the classroom computers.

9 Once the scan has been completed, click OK.

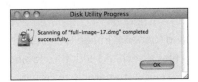

   Your image is now ready for use as a source when restoring
   another computer.

10 Eject the Client computer's hard drive or drag its FireWire drive
   icon to the Trash.

11 Disconnect the Client computer from one end of the FireWire cable.

> **Warning!** Failure to eject a mounted volume before
> disconnecting the FireWire cable could result in data loss
> on the connected volume.

12 Restart the Client computer.

   Because you removed the .AppleSetupDone file earlier, the
   Client computer will play the new intro movie and open the
   Setup Assistant.

13 Repeat the steps to add a new administrator account, "Client
   Administrator" (cadmin, password: cadmin).

   For your reference, the steps to set up the Client computer are
   provided in Exercise 1.1.3.

   If prompted for Managed Preference usage, click Disable
   (enable remember your choice).

   Set the computer name in the Sharing pane of System
   Preferences to "Mac *Number.*"

171

4.2 System Image Utility and Modular System Images

The new features of System Image Utility (SIU) allow system administrators to quickly and easily create system images from packages and installers—instead of cloning existing Client computers. When utilizing this approach, a clean and "generic" image is created that does not have any of the legacy files associated with the cloning method. In addition, the workflow and Automator actions with SIU and, indeed, Automator allow for user interaction and flexibility when creating these types of images.

System Image Utility (SIU)

Installed with the Server Admin tools and only works with Mac OS X v10.6 systems, client or server

Creates three types of network disk images:

▸ **NetBoot**—Full operational system volume

▸ **NetInstall**—Installs a system

▸ **NetRestore**—Restores a system image

From two main sources:

▸ Installation media—Original or disk image

▸ Prepared system—"Model" system volume or disk image

Two system image–creation modes:

▸ Basic mode creates simple images.

▸ Custom mode creates images based on Automator workflows.

For details, see "Understanding System Image Utility (SIU)" in Chapter 4 of *Apple Training Series: Mac OS X Deployment v10.6.*

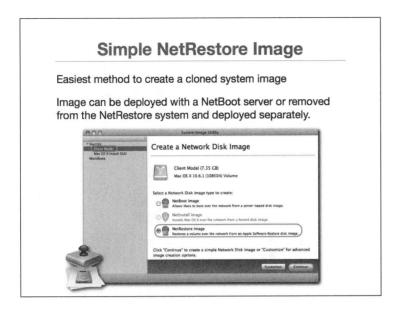

For details, see "Creating Basic Images with SIU" in Chapter 4 of *Apple Training Series: Mac OS X Deployment v10.6.*

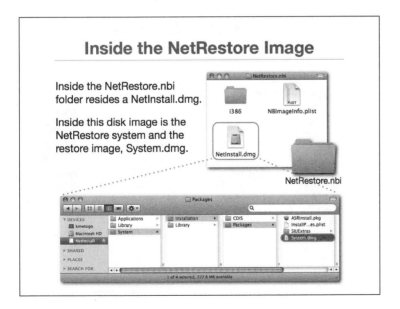

For details, see "Understanding System Image Utility (SIU)" in Chapter 4 of *Apple Training Series: Mac OS X Deployment v10.6.*

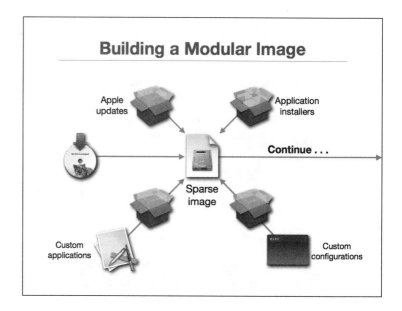

For details, see "Modular Image Overview and Preparation" in Chapter 4 of *Apple Training Series: Mac OS X Deployment v10.6*.

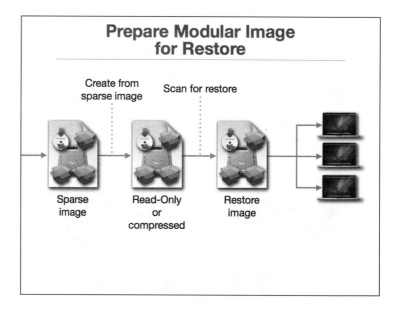

For details, see "Modular Image Overview and Preparation" in Chapter 4 of *Apple Training Series: Mac OS X Deployment v10.6*.

For details, see "Understanding SIU Workflows" in Chapter 4 of
Apple Training Series: Mac OS X Deployment v10.6.

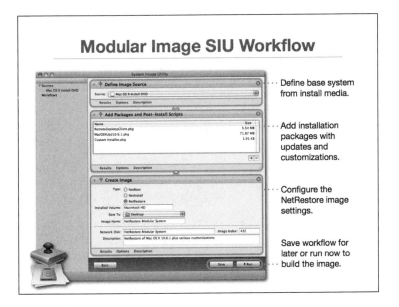

For details, see "Building Modular NetRestore Images with SIU" in
Chapter 4 of *Apple Training Series: Mac OS X Deployment v10.6.*

Comparing Techniques

Cloned system image	Modular restore image
▸ Relies on manual configuration of model computer	▸ Leverages installation packages
– Increases workload, especially with updates	– Uses a standard format
– Auditing based on manual inspection and documentation	– Easy to update
– Requires repetitive "cleaning" and testing	– Can take advantage of scripts
▸ Problematic when deploying to different computer models	– Easily audited
	– Works with a variety of tools
	– Images are already "clean."
	▸ Images are model independent.

For details, see "Understanding System Image Creation" in Chapter 4 of *Apple Training Series: Mac OS X Deployment v10.6.*

Exercise 4.2.1

Build a Modular NetRestore Image Using SIU

Objective

- Use System Image Utility (SIU) to build a modular system image based on the Mac OS X install media, updates, and custom packages

In the previous exercise, you created restore images from existing Macintosh installs—much like most deployment efforts up to this point. When an existing install is used for imaging, several problems can occur: caches may not be removed, network configuration may not be as expected, and cleanup of the install prior to imaging may not be complete.

To combat these issues, you can create a complete system image from installation packages. Furthermore, Apple updates can be added in as they come along, and your own customized packages can be included in the image build.

In this exercise you will set up a system image creation area that will be used for this process, create one more package that includes some of the customizations you have made to your model computer, and create a modular system image.

Prepare Custom Installation Packages and Custom Image Ingredients

You will take the customizations you made to the Client computer and encapsulate them into a custom installation package that can be applied to the system image you create here. Replace *n* with your student number below.

1   On your Server computer, edit the Student Materials/Chapter4/ pcds-startup script file (either use TextWrangler or vi in a Terminal window).

2 Change one of the initial variables in the script:

snum=n

to your student number; so for Student17, the line would look like:

snum=17

3 Save the script and exit Textwrangler/vi.

4 On your Server computer, open PackageMaker, enter com.pretendco for Organization, choose Mac OS X v10.5 Leopard for Minimum Target, and click OK.

5 Give the installation package a title of "custom os *n*."

6 Set the Install Destination to be "Volume selected by user" and verify that User Sees is set to Easy Install Only.

7 Drag the following components from the Student Materials/ Chapter4 folder into the contents window of PackageMaker:

- startup-stuff

- PCDS-background.jpg

- com.pretendco.startup.plist

- pcds-startup

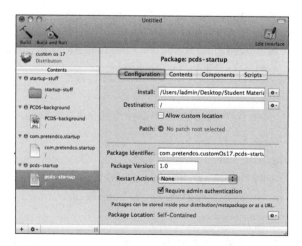

8 Change the destination for startup-stuff to /System/Library/ CoreServices/Setup Assistant.app/Contents/Resources/ TransitionSection.bundle/Contents/Resources/.

> **Note** "Setup Assistant.app" has a space in its name. Do not include the quotation marks; they have been added for clarity.

9 Change the destination for PCDS-background.jpg to /Library/ Desktop Pictures/.

10 Change the Destination for com.pretendco.startup.plist to /Library/LaunchDaemons/.

11 Change the Destination for pcds-startup to /Library/Scripts/.

12 Click the Contents button for com.pretendco.startup.plist and change the ownerships and permissions to:

- Owner: root

- Group: wheel

- Owner has Read and Write permissions

- Group and Others have Read only permission

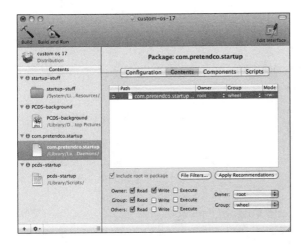

13 Click the Contents button for pcds-startup and change the ownerships and permissions to:

- Owner: root

- Group: wheel

- Owner has Read, Write, and Execute permissions
- Group has Read and Execute permissions
- Others has Read only permission

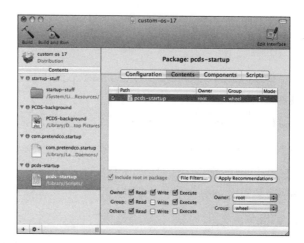

14 Save your project as custom-os-*n* in your ~/Documents/ Packages folder.

15 Click Build.

16 Apply any recommendations and then rebuild if necessary.

17 Save your package as custom-os-*n* also in ~/Documents/ Packages.

18 Close the PackageMaker window and click Save when prompted.

Now that you've created the custom installation package, it's time to gather the other custom installation items.

Add Update and Custom Packages

To customize and update the base OS, you will copy any updates and custom packages into the working area for image creation.

1 In the Finder, open your ~/Documents/Images folder.

2 Copy (Option-drag) any Mac OS X combo or delta updates from the Student Materials/Updates folder into the ~/Documents/ Images folder.

If there is more than one update, ask your instructor which one(s) to use.

> **Note** If any of the updates are contained within a disk image, mount that disk image first and then copy the installation package into ~/Documents/Images.

3 Copy (Option-drag) the custom-os-*n*.pkg from ~/Documents/Packages into ~/Documents/Images.

This is the package you created above that includes custom preference files and scripts to add and then lock down the desktop picture.

You are now ready to create the foundation of your image—your base OS.

Create a Base OS Installer Image from DVD Install Media (optional)

You will use Disk Utility to create an image of your install DVD.

The following steps are not essential to the modular image creation process, but they are recommended if you plan to automate this process and want to place updated base OS disk images into your workflow at a later time.

These steps may have been completed by your instructor; if so, copy the base OS disk image from the classroom's main server in your ~/Documents/Images folder.

If a generic Mac OS X v10.6 install DVD cannot be used with your Client computer, use the install media that came with that computer for the following two sections.

1 Log in to your Server computer as ladmin and open Disk Utility.

2 Insert the Mac OS X Install media into your Server computer's optical drive.

3 In Disk Utility, select the Mac OS X Install DVD from the source list.

4 Choose File > New > Disk Image from the Mac OS X Install DVD.

5 Save your image as BaseOS-10.6.*X*.dmg in ~/Documents/Images.

Replace *X* with the step release number of your install media (for example, BaseOS-10.6.0.dmg).

6 Click Save.

The imaging process will take approx 10 to 40 minutes, depending on the speed of the classroom computers. It will take up approximately 5.2 GB of disk space.

Once the imaging process is complete, you will be ready to move on to the system image creation process.

7 Eject the Mac OS X Install media from your server's optical drive.

Use SIU to Build a Modular NetRestore Image

Your instructor may provide disk images for the following steps instead of installation media.

Follow these steps to install your base OS disk image:

1 On your server, in the Finder open the ~/Documents/Images folder.

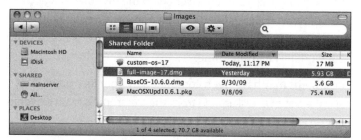

 2 Double-click to mount the BaseOS-10.6.*X*.dmg file.

 3 Open SIU (located in /Applications/Server or on your Dock).

SIU will open and automatically select the Mac OS X Installation DVD source for a NetInstall image.

4 Click the Add (+) button and select Create New Workflow.

5 Click Agree to the License information.

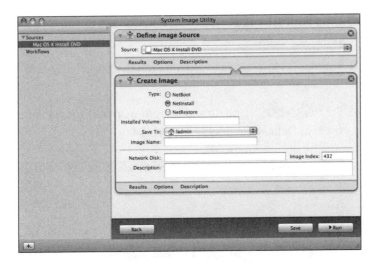

The Define and Create Image actions are already present.

6   Drag the Add Packages and Post-Install Scripts action directly under the Define Image Source action.

7   Click the + (plus) button to add in any system updates from ~/Documents/Images.

8   Click the + (plus) button again to add your custom-os-*n*.pkg custom packages, also from ~/Documents/Images.

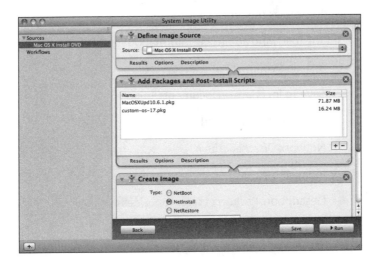

9 Drag the Customize Package Selection action directly under the previous action.

10 For Mac OS X, deselect everything but the Essential System Software.

11 For the Mac OS X Update and custom-os-*n* packages, enable them as Default but disable their visibility.

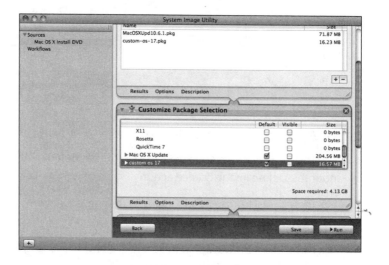

12 Finally, scroll down to the Create Image action and select NetRestore as the type.

13 Set the following additional information for this image:

- Installed volume: PretendcoSystem

- Save To location: ~/Documents/Images

- Image Name: Net-Modular-*n*

- Network Disk: Modular-*n*

- Image Index: 9*n*

- Description: Modular image for client *n*

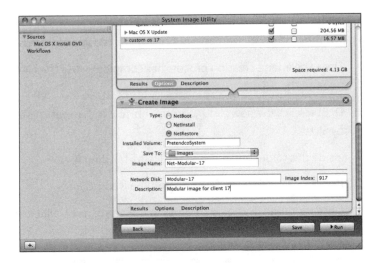

14 Click Save to save this workflow (for future use) as modular-*n* in your ~/Documents/Images folder.

15 Click Save and then click Run to start the image creation process.

16 Authenticate as ladmin.

Depending on the speed of the computers in the classroom, the image creation process could take anywhere from 10 to 50 minutes.

Note If any updates require user interaction, instruct the installer that a command-line install is being executed by running the following command in your shell before installing the update:

```
export COMMAND_LINE_INSTALL=1
```

You have now created a full system image based on installation media, software updates, and custom packages.

The image you have created contains one known user account (hadmin) and no other users. When this image is deployed on your Client computer, the startup video will play, and the Setup Assistant will open.

Examine the Modular Image (optional)

Follow these steps to examine your newly created image:

1 Once the image creation process has completed, use the Finder to open the ~/Documents/Images folder.

2 Double-click the new Net-Modular-*n*.nbi folder that was created by SIU.

3 Inside this folder you will find the NetInstall.dmg file.

4 Double-click this .dmg file to mount the NetInstall OS.

5 Once mounted, navigate through to the /System/Installation/ Packages folder on this NetInstall volume.

6 There you will find the System.dmg file. This is your modular system image that can be used to cleanly restore your Client computer.

7 Drag the System.dmg to your ~/Documents/Images folder and rename it modular_*n*.dmg.

8 Unmount the NetInstall volume.

9 Unmount/eject the Base Mac OS X Install DVD disk image/media.

You will use the modular_*n*.dmg later when restoring your Client computer from alternative sources.

Create a Cloned NetRestore Image Using SIU (optional)

Objective

- Use SIU to build a cloned system image based on your Client computer's installation

As in a previous exercise you created restore images from existing Macintosh installs—much like most deployment efforts up to this point. When an existing install is used for imaging, several problems can occur: caches may not be removed, network configuration may not be as expected, and cleanup of the install prior to imaging may not be complete.

To combat these issues, you can use SIU to create a cloned system image from your Client computer and also remove the client machine–specific files normally associated with this type of imaging process.

Use SIU to Create a Cloned NetRestore Image

You will put your Client computer into target disk mode again (as you did in Exercise 4.1.2) and create a NetRestore image from it. Replace *n* with your student number below.

1 On your Client computer, log in as cadmin and open System Preferences.

2 Click Startup Disk, click the Target Disk Mode button, and click Restart.

   Your Client computer will restart in target disk mode.

3 Connect your Client computer to your server with a FireWire cable.

4 Open SIU, in the main window change the image type to NetRestore, and click Continue.

Your Client computer's boot volume is automatically chosen as the image source.

5 Change the Image Settings to:

- Network Disk: `NetRestore Clone n`

- Description: `NetRestore of Mac OS X 10.6.x from cloned source n.`

6 Click Create and then click Agree.

7 Save your NetRestore image in ~/Documents/Images as `NetRestore clone n`.

8 Click Save and authenticate as ladmin.

The image creation process could take from 10 to 50 minutes, depending on the speed of the classroom computers.

9 Once the image creation is complete, you will have another image folder in ~/Documents/Images.

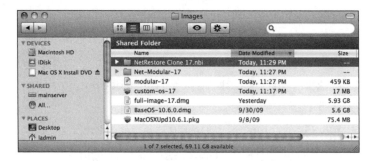

Exercise 4.2.3

Update Your Deployment Planning Template

During the previous exercises, you created a variety of system images that you will use to restore your Client computers using a number of methods in the next chapter.

Because of the time involved in creating these images, you'll want to plan your image creation carefully to minimize rework.

In Exercise 4.2.2 you learned how to make a completely clean full system image. Consider using that method: Automator actions and Services let you easily manage image creation and facilitate easy documentation of your image contents.

Now it's time to update your template to see which of the various methods lend themselves to your particular situation:

- Cloned system images

- Modular system images

When filling out your template, please remember to include the rationale for using these forms of deployment.

5

Deploying System Images

5.1   **System Deployment Overview**

Exercise 5.1.1   Use Disk Utility to Restore an Image Locally

5.2   **Using the NetBoot Service**

Exercise 5.2.1   Configure Initial NetBoot Settings

Exercise 5.2.2   Enable and Test a NetRestore Image

Exercise 5.2.3   Create a Server NetInstall Image (optional)

5.3   **Deploying Systems with NetRestore and NetInstall**

Exercise 5.3.1   Create a Workflow NetInstall Image

Exercise 5.3.2   Enable and Test the NetInstall Image

Exercise 5.3.3   Use NetRestore Images with Alternative Sources

Exercise 5.3.4   Update Your Deployment Planning Template

5.1 System Deployment Overview

Creating system images is only half a solution (although it's generally more complicated than deploying system images). In this lesson you will learn how to use a variety of mechanisms, such as Apple Software Restore (ASR), to efficiently deploy your system image to a local Mac computer. It may seem like this lesson provides an incomplete solution—and it does for most deployment scenarios—but this is to keep the focus on the restore technology. As you'll learn in the next chapter, combining this restore technology with network-based systems provides a more robust system deployment solution.

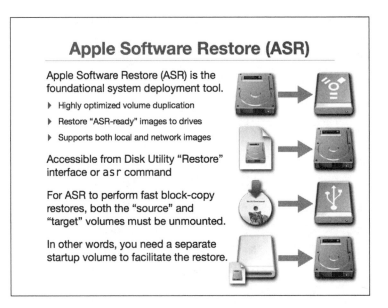

Apple Software Restore (ASR)

Apple Software Restore (ASR) is the foundational system deployment tool.

▸ Highly optimized volume duplication

▸ Restore "ASR-ready" images to drives

▸ Supports both local and network images

Accessible from Disk Utility "Restore" interface or asr command

For ASR to perform fast block-copy restores, both the "source" and "target" volumes must be unmounted.

In other words, you need a separate startup volume to facilitate the restore.

For details, see "Understanding System Image Deployment" in Chapter 5 of *Apple Training Series: Mac OS X Deployment v10.6*.

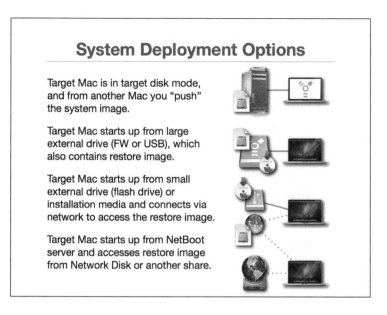

For details, see "Multicast ASR Details" in Chapter 4 of *Apple Training Series: Mac OS X Deployment v10.6.*

For details, see "Restore System Images Locally" in Chapter 5 of *Apple Training Series: Mac OS X Deployment v10.6.*

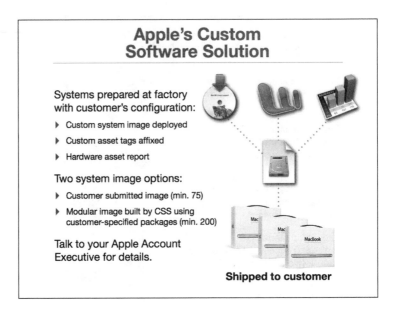

For details, see "Understanding System Image Deployment" in Chapter 5 of *Apple Training Series: Mac OS X Deployment v10.6*.

Exercise 5.1.1

Use Disk Utility to Restore an Image Locally

Objective

- Use an image to restore a client computer that is booted into target disk mode and connected to your server with a FireWire cable

Disk Utility, the same tool you used to create the full system image in Exercise 4.1.2, can be used to restore disk images to computer volumes, too.

Restoration of system volumes in this manner, using Disk Utility, does not require the infrastructure setup for NetBoot services, and it can be executed only one volume at a time.

Place Client Computer in Target Disk Mode and Connect to Server Computer

1 On your Client computer, log in as cadmin and open System Preferences.

2 From the Startup Disk pane, click Target Disk Mode and click Restart (authenticate if necessary).

   Your Client computer will now restart in target disk mode.

3 Connect your Client computer to your Server computer with a FireWire cable.

   Your Client computer is now ready to be restored.

Use Disk Utility to Restore a System Image

You will use Disk Utility to restore the previously created image back onto the Client computer. Replace n with your student number where applicable.

1 On your Server computer, open Disk Utility.

2 Click the Client computer's PretendcoSystem volume and then click Restore.

The Restore window presents options to specify source and destination.

3 Drag the full-image-*n*.dmg from the source list to the Source box.

If your image is not shown in the source list, click Image and navigate to select it from the ~/Documents/Images folder.

The full-image-*n*.dmg system image is the one you created in Exercise 4.1.2.

4 Drag the Client computer's PretendcoSystem folder to the Destination field.

> **Note** If you can't seem to put anything in the Destination field, verify that you are using the correct image, and that it was scanned for restore (during Exercise 4.1.2). If it was not, scan it here using Disk Utility. You may have to quit and restart Disk Utility once the scan is finished for your destination to "stick" properly in the Destination field.

5 Click "Erase destination" and then click Restore.

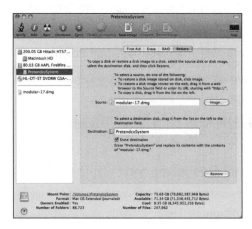

6 Select Erase and then authenticate as ladmin to start the restore process.

The restore and verify process will take approximately 10 to 40 minutes, depending on the speed of the classroom computers.

To restore without verifying, use `diskutil` at the command line.

7 Once the restore has completed, eject the Client computer's volume.

8 Disconnect the FireWire cable from both computers and reboot the Client computer.

Question 1 Did you see a login window on the Client computer?

9 Repeat the setup steps to create a local Client Administrator account on the Client computer.

10 If prompted to connect to Mac OS X Server, click Continue.

Question 2 Does it have the same customizations as before?

11 Open System Preferences and click Sharing.

Question 3 What is the computer name?

Notice the name of your Client computer now. In Chapter 6, you will learn how to apply customizations, such as directory bindings and computer names, to freshly imaged computers.

12 Test logging in as the user hadmin and controlling your Client computer with the hadmin credentials in ARD.

5.2 Using the NetBoot Service

The primary drawback to the built-in Mac OS X restore system is that you cannot restore to a volume that is acting as the current startup volume. Because most Macs have only a single local hard drive, you have to start up the Mac from another system to restore a system image to that local drive. Although you can certainly choose to start up from the installation media or a directly attached external drive, neither of these solutions scales very well.

Enter the Mac OS X Server NetBoot service, which allows you to deliver a system volume to nearly any Mac via the network. In this lesson you will explore the NetBoot architecture and set up the NetBoot service.

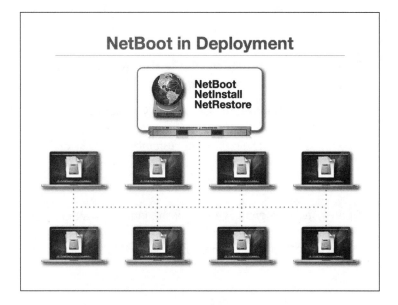

For details, see "Understanding the NetBoot Service" in Chapter 5 of *Apple Training Series: Mac OS X Deployment v10.6*.

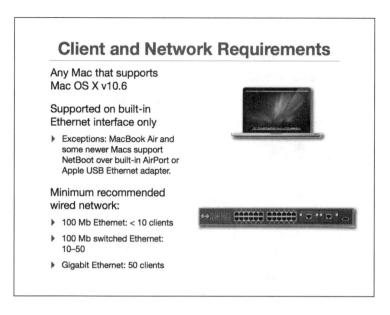

For details, see "Understanding the NetBoot Service" in Chapter 5 of *Apple Training Series: Mac OS X Deployment v10.6*.

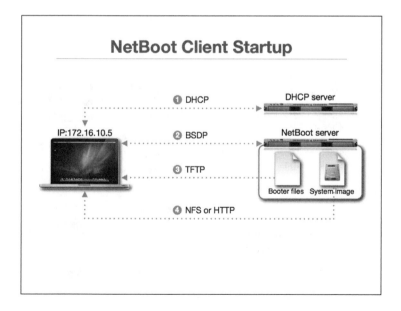

For details, see "Understanding the NetBoot Service" in Chapter 5 of *Apple Training Series: Mac OS X Deployment v10.6*.

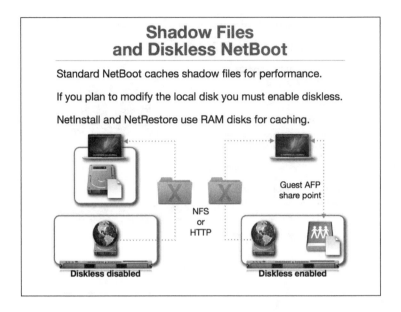

For details, see "Understanding the NetBoot Service" in Chapter 5 of *Apple Training Series: Mac OS X Deployment v10.6.*

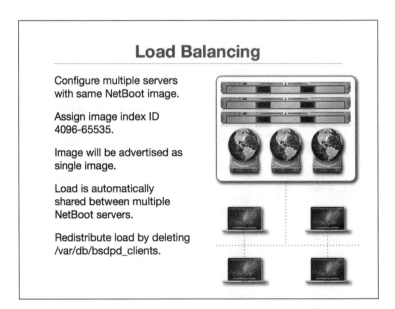

For details, see "Understanding the NetBoot Service" in Chapter 5 of *Apple Training Series: Mac OS X Deployment v10.6.*

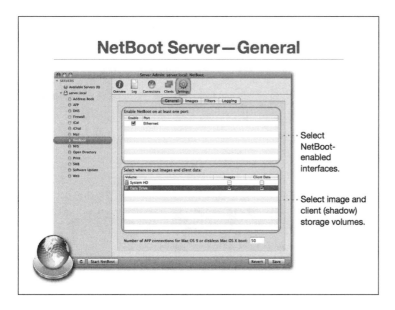

For details, see "Configuring the NetBoot Service" in Chapter 5 of
Apple Training Series: Mac OS X Deployment v10.6.

System Image Utility (SIU)

Installed with the Server Admin tools and only works with
Mac OS X v10.6 systems, client or server

Creates three types of Network Disk images:

▶ **NetBoot**—Full operational system volume

▶ **NetInstall**—Installs a system

▶ **NetRestore**—Restores a system image

From two main sources:

▶ Installation media—Original or disk image

▶ Prepared system—"Model" system volume or disk image

Two system image–creation modes:

▶ Basic mode creates simple images.

▶ Custom mode creates images based on Automator workflows.

For details, see "Understanding System Image Utility (SIU)" in
Chapter 4 of *Apple Training Series: Mac OS X Deployment v10.6.*

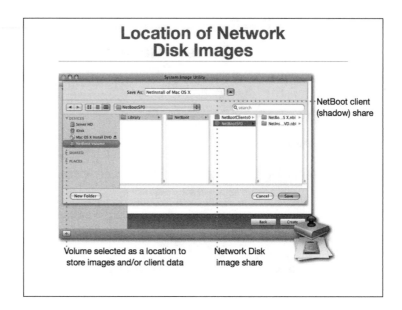

For details, see "Configuring the NetBoot Service" in Chapter 5 of *Apple Training Series: Mac OS X Deployment v10.6*.

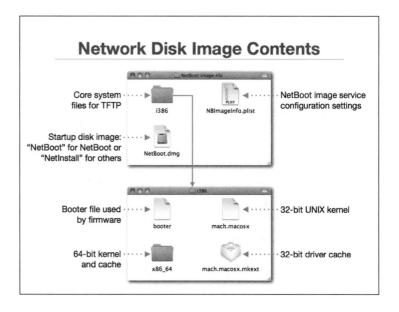

For details, see "Understanding the NetBoot Service" in Chapter 5 of *Apple Training Series: Mac OS X Deployment v10.6*.

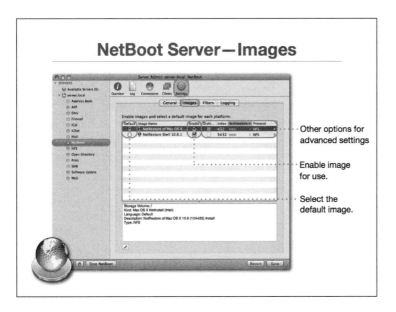

For details, see "Configuring the NetBoot Service" in Chapter 5 of
Apple Training Series: Mac OS X Deployment v10.6.

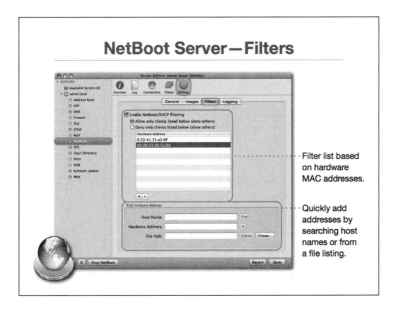

For details, see "Configuring the NetBoot Service" in Chapter 5 of
Apple Training Series: Mac OS X Deployment v10.6.

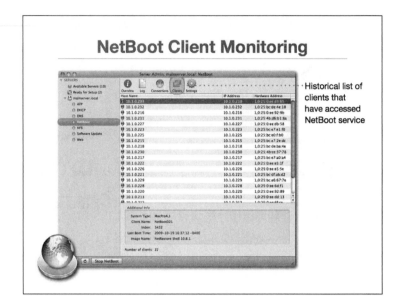

For details, see "Monitoring and Troubleshooting the NetBoot Service" in Chapter 5 of *Apple Training Series: Mac OS X Deployment v10.6.*

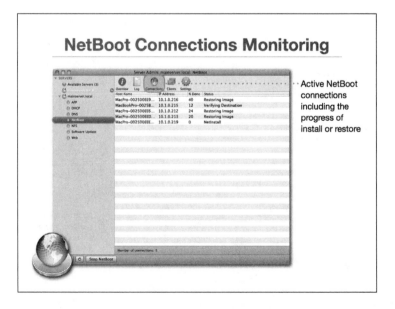

For details, see "Monitoring and Troubleshooting the NetBoot Service" in Chapter 5 of *Apple Training Series: Mac OS X Deployment v10.6.*

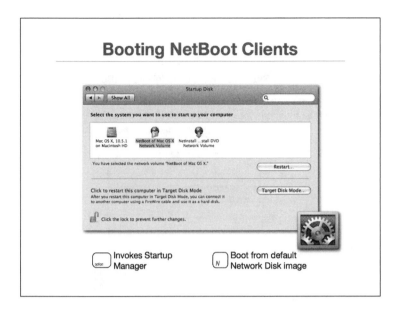

For details, see "Configuring Clients to NetBoot" in Chapter 5 of
Apple Training Series: Mac OS X Deployment v10.6.

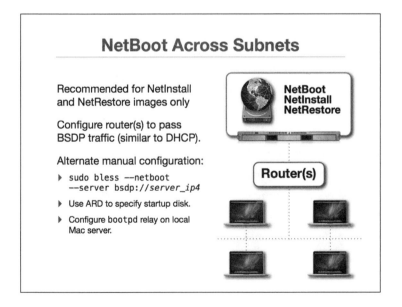

For details, see "Configuring Clients to NetBoot" in Chapter 5 of
Apple Training Series: Mac OS X Deployment v10.6.

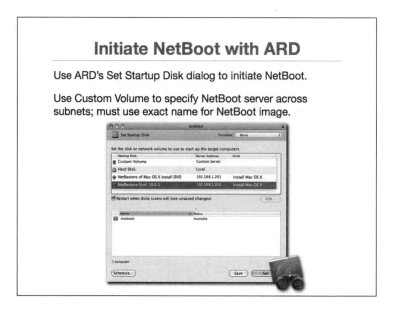

For details, see "Configuring Clients to NetBoot" in Chapter 5 of
Apple Training Series: Mac OS X Deployment v10.6.

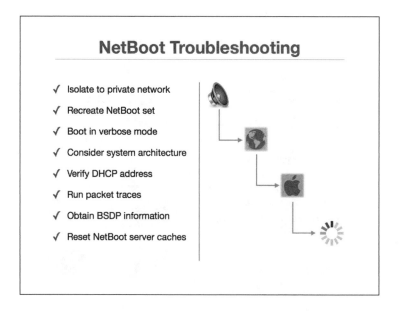

For details, see "Monitoring and Troubleshooting the NetBoot Service"
in Chapter 5 of *Apple Training Series: Mac OS X Deployment v10.6.*

Exercise 5.2.1
Configure Initial NetBoot Settings

Objective

- Set up initial NetBoot service settings that will create the NetBoot share points

These are the first steps towards using NetBoot to start up with a network-based Mac OS X image. When using NetBoot, your client machines obtain a fresh copy of the operating system from your NetBoot server. Advanced configurations include the use of the client machine's local hard drive or network share point for swap and cache storage. For performance reasons, we'll use the Client computer's hard drive for these purposes now.

In addition to NetBoot images, you can create NetInstall and NetRestore images from which a client machine may boot and obtain software, system, or custom files—these are copied directly to the client machine's hard drive. You will be using NetInstall and NetRestore images later.

Initial Setup of NetBoot Services

Unless you have configured the NetBoot server to start automatically, there is no NetBoot share point inside /Library. This is where images are stored by default. You will partially configure NetBoot services to create this share point.

1 On the server, log in as ladmin, open Server Admin, and connect to your server.

2 Select the NetBoot service.

3 Click Settings and, under General settings, enable NetBoot for your server's Ethernet port.

> **Note** If you are working on a computer with more than one Ethernet port, select the appropriate port for the NetBoot service to run on.

4   Select to put images and client machine data on the startup volume for your server.

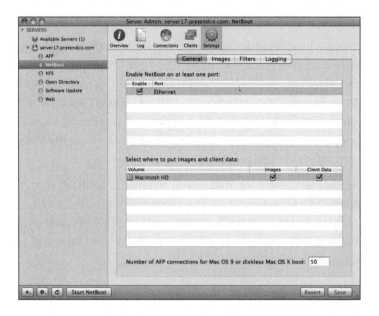

5   Click Save.

6   Select your server's entry on the left and click the File Sharing icon in the toolbar.

7   Check to make sure you have two new share points listed: NetBootClients0 and NetBootSP0.

8   Quit Server Admin.

You don't need to start NetBoot services at this time.

Because you have already used System Image Utility (SIU) to create a couple of images already, you will test those images next.

Exercise 5.2.2
Enable and Test a NetRestore Image

Objective

- Start NetBoot services and use NetBoot to boot a client machine from a NetRestore image

You built a modular NetRestore image in Exercise 4.2.2. You will copy that image into the /Library/NetBoot folder. Then you can finish setting up NetBoot services and start up your Client computer.

Start NetBoot Services

Since you have already partially configured NetBoot services, you have a NetBoot folder share point inside /Library. This is where images are stored by default.

1   On your server, navigate to your ~/Documents/Images folder.

2   Open a second Finder window and navigate to the /Library/ NetBoot/NetBootSP0 folder.

3   Drag both your Net-Modular-*n*.nbi and NetRestore Clone *n*.nbi folders from ~/Documents/Images to the /Library/NetBoot/ NetBootSP0 folder.

4   Once the copy completes, open Server Admin and return to the NetBoot service pane.

5   Click Settings and then click Images.

6   Enable the Modular-*n* image (where *n* is your student number), but do not set it as the default.

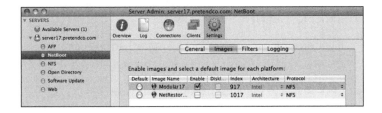

Your new NetRestore image appears in the list of available NetBoot images.

> **Note** Using a NetRestore image as the default could lead to data loss on client computers if they accidentally use NetBoot to boot from this image and proceed with the install/imaging.

7 Click Save and start the NetBoot service.

Filter NetBoot Services

Because all students will be using NetBoot at roughly the same time, you will switch on filtering to restrict your Client computer to NetBoot from your server only.

1 In Server Admin on your Server computer, return to the NetBoot services pane.

2 Click Settings and then click Filters.

3 Enable NetBoot/DHCP filtering and select "Allow only clients listed below (deny others)."

4 Click the plus sign and type in the MAC address for your Client computer's primary Ethernet port.

5 Click OK to add it to the filter list.

If you are going to use NetBoot for more than one computer, add the MAC address for each additional computer to the filter list too.

6 Click Save and then restart NetBoot services.

Start Up Client Machine from a NetRestore Image Using ARD

Once the NetBoot service is running and an image is selected, use Apple Remote Desktop (ARD) from your Server computer to start up the Client computer.

1   On your Server computer, open Remote Desktop.

2   Verify that you can control and observe your Client computer.

3   Select your Client computer in the lab1 computer list and choose Manage > Set Startup Disk.

4   Click the Custom Volume entry and enter the following information (replacing *n* with your student number):

Server: `10.1.`*n*`.1`

Volume name: `Modular-`*n*

5   Click OK.

6   Select "Restart when done" and then click Set.

Once the Client computer restarts from the NetRestore image, you will see the restore process execute.

> **Note** If the first part of this ARD task fails, your Client computer will still restart. Verify that you can control and observe your Client computer before trying this task again.

The installation should take between 20 and 30 minutes depending on the hardware used and network bandwidth available.

7   When the NetRestore operation is complete, click Restart to reboot the Client computer.

The next few steps guide you through setting up the Client computer again and observing the different customizations that have been added from the custom package.

8   As this is a "custom clean" install, go through the Setup Assistant once more to create the local Client Administrator account and observe the desktop that is used for this new account.

9   Log out of the cadmin account.

10 Log in as hadmin.

11 Open System Preferences and click Sharing.

12 Set the Client computer name to Mac *Number* (where *Number* is your student number spelled out).

Computer name and binding to a Directory Server were not part of the installation mechanism that was used to create this NetInstall image.

You will see how to add additional startup customizations, such as these, in Chapter 6.

Exercise 5.2.3
Create a Server NetInstall Image (optional)

Objective

- Use System Image Utility to create a NetInstall image from Mac OS X Server install media

When a Client computer boots from a NetInstall image, a cut-down version of the operating system is running within the image from which the standard Apple Installer application is set to run.

In this exercise you will create a NetInstall image from the Mac OS X Server install media for use in later exercises. Replace *n* with your student number where applicable.

> **Note** This exercise may have been completed by your instructor, with a NetInstall image available on the instructor's server.

Create a NetInstall Image with SIU

1 Insert the Mac OS X Server v10.6 Install DVD into your Server computer's optical drive.

2 Open System Image Utility (SIU).

   The Mac OS X Server Install Disc is selected as the source for your image.

3 Verify that NetInstall Image is selected and click Continue.

4 Enter the following values (where *n* is your student number):

   - Image Name: `Server NetInstall n`
   - Description: `NetInstall of Mac OS X Server 10.6 - server n.`

5   Click Create and click Agree when prompted.

6   In the Save dialog, select /Library/NetBoot/NetBootSP0/ as the
    location for saving this image.

7   Click Save.

8   Authenticate as ladmin when prompted.

    Image creation could take from 40 minutes to over an hour
    depending on the hardware used and size of the image
    being created.

9   Once the image creation process is complete, click Done.

10 Quit SIU and eject the Mac OS X Server Install DVD.

    You have successfully created a NetInstall image that you will
    use later to restore a server.

Deploying Systems with NetRestore and NetInstall

5.3

Once you have a fundamental understanding of the NetBoot service, you can start to take advantage of its advanced deployment features. New to Mac OS X v10.6 is the ability to create more flexible workflow images for NetInstall and NetRestore that, through the use of Automator actions, can be used to automate many system deployment tasks.

You have used some of the more common Automation actions during Exercise 4.2.2. Here you will learn about more of these NetBoot-related Automator actions and build a custom workflow NetBoot image to deploy a system to your Client computer.

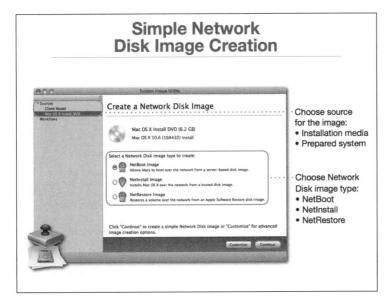

For details, see "Creating Basic Images with SIU" in Chapter 4 of *Apple Training Series: Mac OS X Deployment v10.6.*

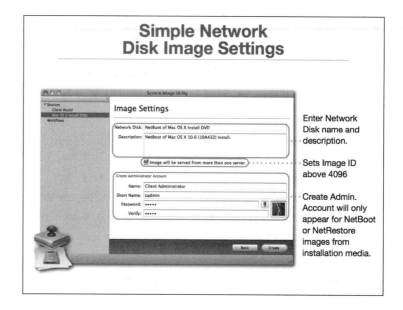

For details, see "Creating Basic Images with SIU" in Chapter 4 of
Apple Training Series: Mac OS X Deployment v10.6.

Simple SIU Build Results

	NetBoot image	NetInstall image	NetRestore image
Installation media	Clients start to full generic system.	Clients start to default Mac OS X installer interface.	Clients start to an interface that will restore a generic system image.
Prepared system	Clients start to full system based on selected source.		Clients start to an interface that will restore a system image based on selected source.

For details, see "Creating Basic Images with SIU" in Chapter 4 of
Apple Training Series: Mac OS X Deployment v10.6.

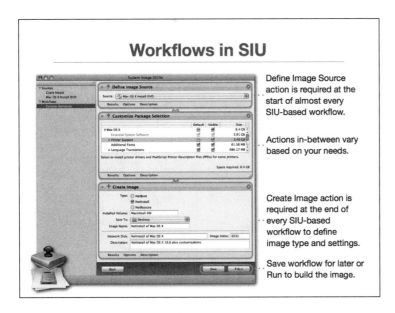

For details, see "Using SIU Workflow Actions" in Chapter 5 of
Apple Training Series: Mac OS X Deployment v10.6.

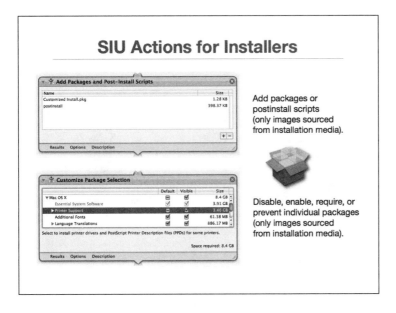

For details, see "Using SIU Workflow Actions" in Chapter 5 of
Apple Training Series: Mac OS X Deployment v10.6.

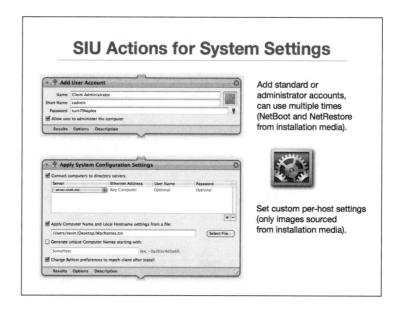

For details, see "Using SIU Workflow Actions" in Chapter 5 of
Apple Training Series: Mac OS X Deployment v10.6.

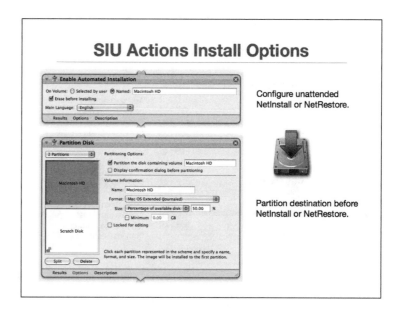

For details, see "Using SIU Workflow Actions" in Chapter 5 of
Apple Training Series: Mac OS X Deployment v10.6.

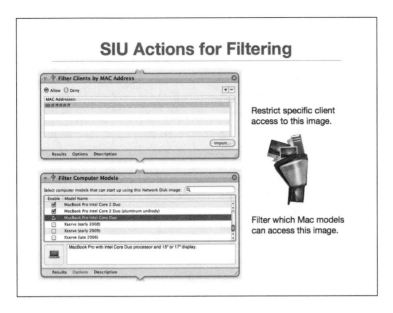

For details, see "Using SIU Workflow Actions" in Chapter 5 of
Apple Training Series: Mac OS X Deployment v10.6.

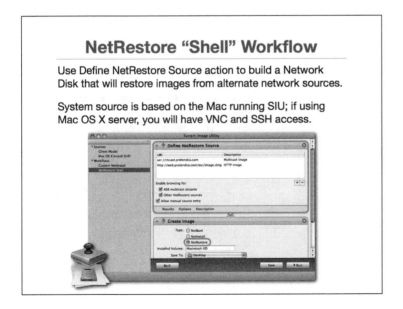

For details, see "Deploying System Images with NetInstall and
NetRestore" in Chapter 5 of *Apple Training Series: Mac OS X
Deployment v10.6.*

SIU Automator Action Usage

SIU Automator Action	NetBoot	NetInstall	NetRestore
Define Image Source (often required)	✓	✓	✓
Create Image (required)	✓	✓	✓
Add Packages and Post-Install Scripts	✓	✓	✓ *
Customize Package Selection	✓	✓	✓
Add User Account	✓	Not Applicable	✓
Apply System Configuration Settings	✓	✓ *	✓ *
Enable Automated Installation	Not Applicable	✓	✓ *
Partition Disk	Not Applicable	✓	
Filter Clients by MAC Address	✓	✓	✓
Filter Computer Models	✓	✓	✓
Define NetRestore Source	Not Applicable	Not Applicable	✓

For details, see "Using SIU Workflow Actions" in Chapter 5 of *Apple Training Series: Mac OS X Deployment v10.6.*

Using SIU Actions with Automator

SIU actions can be integrated with other actions in Automator.

In Automator, SIU actions are found in the System actions.

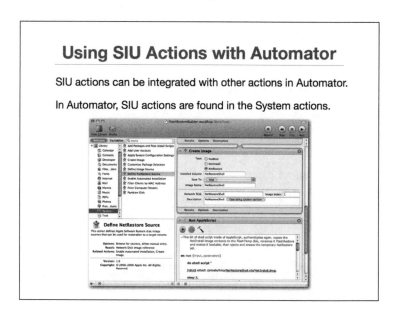

For details, see "Using SIU Workflow Actions" in Chapter 5 of *Apple Training Series: Mac OS X Deployment v10.6.*

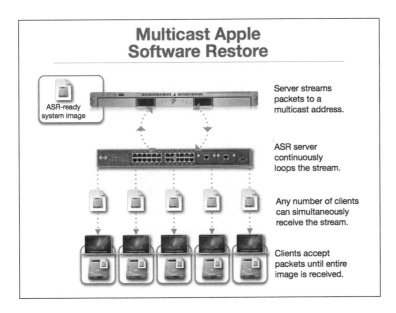

For details, see "Configuring ASR Network Multicast" in Chapter 5 of *Apple Training Series: Mac OS X Deployment v10.6.*

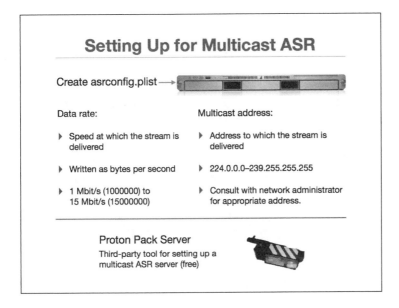

For details, see "Configuring ASR Network Multicast" in Chapter 5 of *Apple Training Series: Mac OS X Deployment v10.6.*

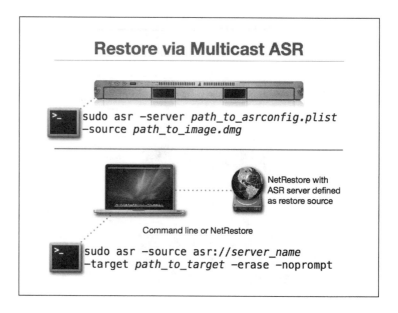

For details, see "Configuring ASR Network Multicast" in Chapter 5 of *Apple Training Series: Mac OS X Deployment v10.6*.

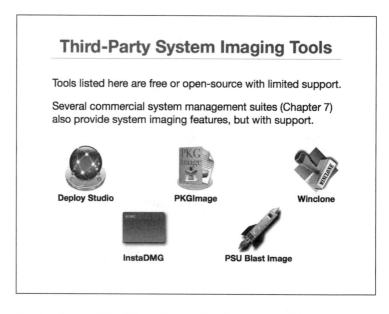

For details, see "Third-Party System Deployment Tools" in Chapter 5 of *Apple Training Series: Mac OS X Deployment v10.6*.

Exercise 5.3.1
Create a Workflow NetInstall Image

Objective

- Use Automator to create a NetInstall image that incorporates workflow actions

As of Mac OS X v10.5, SIU includes the option to add Automator-style workflow actions during the imaging process. As of Mac OS X v10.6, these Automator workflow actions can also be used with Otto, the Automator.app.

In this exercise you will use the BaseOS-10.6.*X*.dmg and add workflow actions to streamline the NetInstall process. You will use Automator to create a NetInstall image that will erase the disk and install Mac OS X 10.6.

Create a Workflow NetInstall Image with Automator

1   On your server, navigate to the ~/Documents/Images folder.

2   Double-click the BaseOS-10.6.*X*.dmg to mount it.

3   Right-click/Control-click your modular-*n* workflow (also in this folder).

4   Select to open with Automator (the default).

    The existing workflow you created with SIU is now available within Automator as a fully customizable workflow.

5   From the File menu, choose Save As and save this as a new work-flow called netinstall-mod-*n* in your ~/Documents/Images folder.

6   From the Library of actions, drag the Ask For Text action to the top of your workflow.

7   In the Question field, enter: `NetInstall image name`.

8   In the Default Answer field, enter: `NI-Modular-`*n*.

9   Enable "Require an answer."

10 Drag the Set Value of Variable action from the Action library to under the previous action.

11 Click the New Variable item within this action and label the new variable: `image name`.

12 Click Done.

13 From the Library of actions, drag the Ask For Text action to under the previous action.

14 In the Question field, enter: `If image will be used on multiple NetBoot servers, enter an image index of 4096 or above.`

15 Enable "Require an answer."

16 Right-click the title for this action and choose Ignore Input.

17 Drag the Set Value of Variable action from the Action library to under the previous action.

18 Click the New Variable item within this action and label the new variable: `image index.`

19 Click Done.

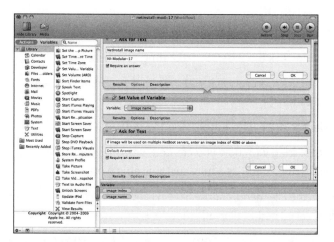

20 Drag the Partition Disk action directly under the Define Image Source action.

Without the Partition Disk action, the NetInstall process would retain existing settings such as user account information and home folders on the destination computer.

21 Change the Name to PretendcoSystem.

22 Scroll down your workflow to the Customize Package Selection action.

23 In the Customize Package Selection action, make the all the Mac OS X packages visible.

24 Drag the Apply System Configuration Settings action under the Custom Package Selection item in your workflow.

25 In the Finder, edit the Student Materials/Chapter5/computer_naming.txt file to include the mac-address of your Client computer's Ethernet port and replace *n* with your student number as shown:

The computer_naming.txt file is a tab-delimited file used to name your computer during the NetInstall process.

26 Enable "Apply Computer Name and Local Hostname settings from a file" and select the Student Materials/Chapter5/computer_naming.txt file.

27 Enable Change ByHost preferences.

28 Scroll down to the Create Image action and change the image type to NetInstall.

29 Change the Image Name setting to the variable "image name."

You can drag and drop the Automator Variable into the Image Name field.

30 Change the Network Disk setting to the variable "image name."

31 Change the Image Index to the variable "image index."

32 Change the description to: NetInstall image for Client *n*.

33 Save your workflow.

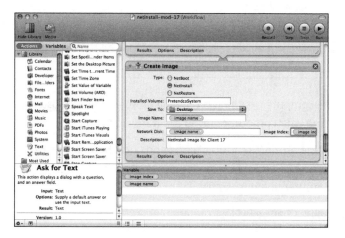

You now have a workflow that can be reused for making your modular system images.

34 Click Run now and enter the image name when prompted: `NI-Modular-n.`

35 When prompted for the Image Index, enter: `11n.`

36 Authenticate as ladmin.

37 When the workflow has finished, quit Automator and unmount the BaseOS-10.6.*X*.dmg.

Create a NetInstall Service with Automator (optional)

Continuing on from the last exercise steps, you can make a service from your automator workflow.

1 On your server, open Automator, select Service from the templates, and click Choose.

2 Change the "Service receives selected" from "text" to "files or folders."

3 Drag the mounted disk image from the desktop to the work-flow area.

4 Next, drag your netinstall-mod-*n* workflow from ~/Documents/Images onto the workflow space.

5 From the File menu, choose Save As.

6 Label this new service as: `create-modular-ni-image`.

   The default location for saving services of this type is ~/Library/Services.

7 Click Save and quit Automator.

8 In the Finder, navigate to your ~/Documents/Images folder and right-click the BaseOS-10.6.*X*.dmg file.

9 From the submenu, select create-modular-ni-image (your new service is listed at the bottom).

10 The disk image mounts, and you are prompted to enter a name for the new NetInstall Image.

11 If you want to test this new service and create yet another new modular NetInstall image, enter: `NI-Modular-n-b` for the image name and `12n` for the image index.

12 Authenticate as ladmin.

   At the conclusion of this workflow, you will have another NetInstall image created in ~/Documents/Images.

Exercise 5.3.2

Enable and Test the NetInstall Image

Objective

- Enable the NetInstall image and use NetBoot to boot a client from a NetInstall image

Now that you have a NetInstall image, you can enable it and start up your Client computer.

Enable the NetInstall Image

Because you have already configured NetBoot services, all you have to do here is enable your newly created image.

1   On your server, navigate to your ~/Documents/Images folder.

2   Drag your new NetInstall image from this folder to the /Library/NetBoot/NetBootSP0 folder.

3   Open Server Admin and return to the NetBoot service pane.

4   Click Settings and then click Images.

5   Enable your new NetInstall (NI-Modular-*n*) image (where *n* is your student number) and set it as the default.

Your new NetInstall image appears in the list of available NetBoot images.

> **Note** Using a NetInstall image as the default could lead to data loss on Client computers if they accidentally use Net-Boot to boot from this image and proceed with the install.

6   Click Save and restart the NetBoot service.

Start Up Client from the NetInstall Image Using ARD

Once the NetBoot service has restarted, use ARD from your Server computer to start up the Client computer.

1   On your Server computer, open Remote Desktop.

2   Verify that you can control and observe your Client computer.

3   Select your Client computer in the lab1 computer list and choose Manage > Set Startup Disk.

4   Double-click Custom Volume and enter `NI-Modular-n` for the boot volume name.

> **Note** You cannot select a NetBoot volume (as a startup disk) using ARD on the same server from which said NetBoot volume is being served—you must type the name in manually using the Custom Volume entry.

5   Select "Restart when done" and then click Set.

Once the Client computer restarts from the NetInstall image, you will see the installation process execute.

> **Note** If the first part of this ARD task fails, your Client computer will still restart. Verify that you can control and observe your Client computer before trying this task again.

With the NetInstall image you created, you will step through some of the installation choices to see the effect of using the workflow actions in the previous exercise.

6 Select English for the language.

7 In the Install Mac OS X screen, click Continue and click Agree when prompted with the License information.

8 Select the PretendcoSystem for the destination and click Customize.

9 Expand the disclosure triangle next to Mac OS X (the first package name listed).

10 Deselect the following packages:

- Printer Support

- Additional Fonts

- Language Translations

- X11

- Rosetta

- QuickTime 7 (you will be installing this on a select list of computers later)

Be sure to keep the additional packages selected (such as the combo/delta update and your custom-os package).

11 Click OK and click Install to start the installation process.

The installation should take between 20 and 40 minutes depending on the hardware used and network bandwidth available.

You may proceed with the next exercise while this installation is in progress. Remember to return and complete these final steps once the installation has completed.

12 When the NetInstall operation is complete, click Restart to reboot the Client computer.

The next few steps guide you through setting up the Client computer again and observing the different customizations that have been added from the custom package.

13 As this is a "custom clean" install, go through the Setup Assistant once more to create the local Client Administrator account and observe the desktop that is used for this new account.

14 Log out of the cadmin account.

15 Log in as hadmin.

16 Open System Preferences and click Sharing.

17 Set the Client computer name to Mac *Number* (where *Number* is your student number spelled out).

Again, computer naming and binding were not part of the installation mechanism that was used to create this NetInstall image.

You will see how to add additional startup customizations, such as these, in Chapter 6.

Exercise 5.3.3

Use NetRestore Images with Alternative Sources

Objectives

- Create two sources for system images: from a web server and from an ASR stream

- Create a NetRestore image that accesses these system source images

- NetBoot a client from the NetRestore image and select which source to use

Now that you are more familiar with NetRestore and workflow images, you will create a new NetRestore image that allows the operator to choose the image for client system restore while NetBooted.

Before you build this flexible NetRestore image, you need to set up your two different sources. You will do that now.

Set Up the Web Server

You will move the modular-*n*.dmg file you created earlier to your web server's root document folder and enable web services.

1   On your Server, open Server Admin and add the web service for your server.

2   Click the newly added web service and click the Start Web Service button.

    Minimal configuration of web services is required for this exercise.

3   In the Finder, move the modular-*n*.dmg file from ~/Documents/Images to the /Library/WebServer/Documents folder. Authenticate as necessary.

    Next you will start an ASR stream, based on a different .dmg file.

Set Up the ASR Multicast Server

You will use ASR multicast to share an image over the network for distribution. Then you will use the `asr` command on the Client computer to restore the Client computer's hard drive.

1   On your Server computer, in the Finder, move your full-image-*n*.dmg file from ~/Documents/Images to a new folder called ~/Documents/asr_images.

2   Open Terminal.

3   Use the following two commands to create a configuration file for ASR, where *n* is your student number:

```
defaults write ~/Documents/asr_images/asrconfig \
"Data Rate" -int 2000000
```

```
defaults write ~/Documents/asr_images/asrconfig \
"Multicast Address" 224.0.0.n0
```

These two commands create a configuration file that sets up ASR to multicast at a data rate of approximately 1.86 MB per second over 224.0.0.*n*0.

These values were based on a private gigabit network using mid- to low-range computers (Mac Minis and MacBooks). Consult with your network administrator to find appropriate values for your ASR server.

4   Use the following command to set the permissions on the newly created asrconfig.plist file:

```
chmod og=rw ~/Documents/asr_images/asrconfig.plist
```

5   In Terminal, type the following command to start ASR multicast. Do this on your Server computer only if the instructor tells you it's OK.

```
sudo asr -source ~/Documents/asr_images/\
full-image-n.dmg -server \
~/Documents/asr_images/asrconfig.plist
```

6   Authenticate as ladmin when requested. If all is well, you will see:

```
Ready to start accepting clients
```

7   The full-image-*n*.dmg is the ASR-ready disk image you created in Exercise 4.1.2. Now this image can be accessed on the network for multicast distributions.

The instructor will designate which server will be used to provide the ASR multicast stream to the entire class.

8   If your Server computer is not designated to provide the ASR multicast stream, and you had started an ASR multicast, press Control-C in Terminal to stop the `asr` command.

Create a NetRestore "Shell" Image

Next, you will create a NetRestore "shell" image that will be used to NetBoot your Client computer and allow it to select an image source to use.

1   On your Server, open SIU and create a new workflow.

2   Click Agree and remove any actions that may have prepopulated your new workflow.

3   Drag the Define NetRestore Source from the action library.

4   Click the + (plus) button to add a new URI.

5   Enter the following information for your new URI:

   • URI: `asr://servern.pretendco.com`

   • Description: multicast image

6   Click the + (plus) button to add a new URI.

7   Enter the following information for your new URI:

   • URI: `http://servern.pretendco.com/modular_n.dmg`

   • Description: `webserver image`

8   Enable browsing for both ASR multicast streams, for Other NetRestore sources and Allow manual source entry.

9   Drag the Create Image action to your workflow as your next and final action.

10 Choose NetRestore as the image type.

11 Use the following information to complete the settings for Create Image:

- Save to: NetBootSP0 (the default)

- Image Name: `NetRestore Flex` n

- Network Disk: `NetRestore Flex` n

- Description: `Flexible NetRestore Image` n

- Image Index: `20`n

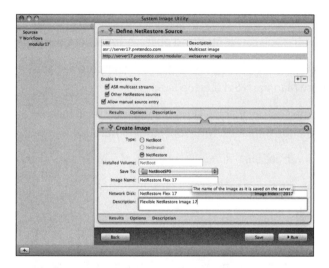

12 Save your workflow as Flex-NR-n in ~/Documents/Images and click Run.

13 Authenticate as ladmin.

14 Once the image has been created, quit Automator.

15 Open Server Admin and click the NetBoot service.

16 Click the Images button, enable the new NetRestore image, and set it as the default.

Your new flexible NetRestore image appears in the list of available NetBoot images.

17 Click Save and restart the NetBoot service.

Start Up Client from the NetRestore "Shell" Image Using ARD

Once the NetBoot service has restarted, use ARD from your Server computer to start up the Client computer.

1 On your Server computer, open Remote Desktop.

2 Verify that you can control and observe your Client computer.

3 Select your Client computer in the lab1 computer list and choose Manage > Set Startup Disk.

4 Click the Custom Volume button and enter the following information (replace *n* with your student number):

   • Server: `10.1.`*n*`.1`

   • Volume name: `NetRestore Flex `*n*

5 Click OK.

6 Select "Restart when done" and then click Set.

Once the Client computer restarts from the NetRestore image, you will see the installation process execute.

With the NetRestore image you created, you will step through some of the installation choices to select your source image (from web server or ASR).

> **Note** Two instances of the mASR stream may appear in the NetRestore interface. This is because one was manually configured by you and the other is being discovered via Bonjour.

7 Select the web server-based image and click Continue.

8 As this is a "custom clean" install, go through the Setup Assistant once more to create the local Client Administrator account and observe the desktop that is used for this new account.

9   On your client machine, log out of the cadmin account.

10 Log in as hadmin.

11 Open System Preferences, click Sharing, and set your computer name to "Pretendco Client *n*".

Restore Client Computer Using ASR (optional)

As an alternative from pulling the source restore image from a website, you can also choose to restore from an ASR multicast stream.

Confirm with your instructor as to whether you should proceed with this exercise.

1   On your Server computer, open Remote Desktop.

2   Verify that you can control and observe your Client computer.

3   Select your Client computer in the lab1 computer list and choose Manage > Set Startup Disk.

4   Click the Custom Volume button and enter the following information (replacing *n* with your student number):

   - Server: `10.1.n.1`

   - Volume name: `NetRestore Flex n`

5   Click OK.

6   Select "Restart when done" and then click Set.

   With the NetRestore image you created, you will step through some of the installation choices to select your source image (from web server or ASR).

7   Select the ASR URI for restore image and click Continue.

8   Wait until the image restore is complete and then restart your Client computer.

9   As this is a cleaned-up "full-image" install, you will need to go through the Setup Assistant once more to create the local Client Administrator account.

Exercise 5.3.4

Update Your Deployment Planning Template

During the previous exercises, you have examined the infrastructure and necessary steps to deploy complete system images across the network.

Whether you are booting from a centralized operating system available from your NetBoot Server or installing a copy of the operating system using a NetInstall image, you need to follow certain steps to prepare.

Careful planning for the types, quantity, and frequency of image creation should be at the top of your list when considering a deployment solution involving these technologies.

The time has come once again to update your template to see which of the various network deployment methods lend themselves to your particular situation:

- NetBoot images

- NetInstall images

- Workflow NetBoot/NetInstall images

When filling out your template, please remember to include the rationale for using these forms of deployment.

6

Postimaging Deployment Considerations

6.1 Postimaging Client Configuration

Exercise 6.1.1 Update Client Settings Using ARD
Exercise 6.1.2 Configure Automated Scripts
Exercise 6.1.3 Install Packages Automatically from a Server

6.2 Postimaging Server Configuration

Exercise 6.2.1 Use the Automatic Server Setup System
Exercise 6.2.2 Update Your Deployment Planning Template

6.1 Postimaging Client Configuration

There is no doubt that deploying a consistent system image to all your clients is a huge time saver, but there is a catch: You cannot simply deploy an identical configuration to all your computers. At the very least, you will need to configure unique network information for your Macintosh computers, and for most deployments there are often many more settings that should be unique. In this lesson you will explore methods to deploy postimaging client configurations as quickly as possible or, ideally, in a completely automated manner.

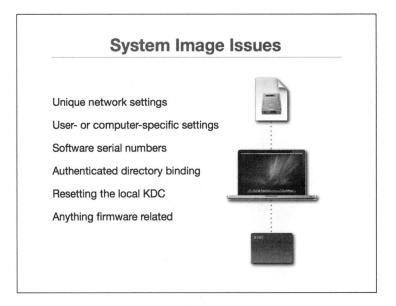

For details, see "Understanding Postimaging Client Configuration" in Chapter 6 of *Apple Training Series: Mac OS X Deployment v10.6.*

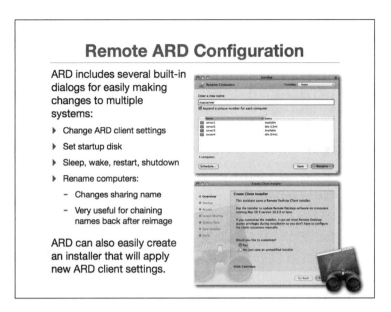

For details, see "Configuration via ARD" in Chapter 6 of *Apple Training Series: Mac OS X Deployment v10.6.*

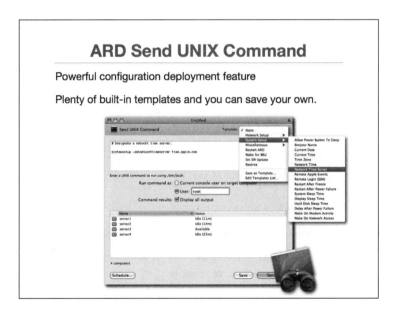

For details, see "Configuration via ARD" in Chapter 6 of *Apple Training Series: Mac OS X Deployment v10.6.*

Command-Line Configuration

systemsetup—Computer system settings (power, computer name, time, SSH, etc.)

▸ `systemsetup -setnetworktimeserver servername`

networksetup—Primary network configuration

▸ `networksetup -setmanual "Ethernet" 10.1.n.2
  255.255.0.0 10.1.0.1`

kickstart—Uninstall, install, activate, or configure ARD

▸ `sudo /System/Library/CoreServices/RemoteManagement
  /ARDAgent.app/Contents/Resources/kickstart -configure
  -allowAccessFor -allUsers -privs -all`

For details, see "System Configuration via Command Line" in Chapter 6 of *Apple Training Series: Mac OS X Deployment v10.6.*

Directory Service Configuration

Reset the local KDC if you need authenticated OD bindings:

▸ `sudo rm -fr /var/db/krb5kdc`

▸ `sudo security delete-keychain /Library/Keychains
  /System.keychain`

▸ `sudo /usr/libexec/configureLocalKDC`

dsconfigldap—Configure LDAP binding (including OD):

▸ `sudo dsconfigldap -a server_name -c client_name
  -n config_name -u dir_admin -p dir_pass`

dsconfigad—Configure binding to Active Directory:

▸ `sudo dsconfigad -domain ad_domain_name -a client_name
  -ou "CN=container,DC=domain" -u dir_admin -p dir_pass`

dscl—Interactive directory service browser/editor:

▸ `dscl options datasource command`

For details, see "System Configuration via Command Line" in Chapter 6 of *Apple Training Series: Mac OS X Deployment v10.6.*

Set Firmware Password

Set the firmware password on an admin computer first:

▸ Copy /Volumes/Mac OS X Install DVD/Applications/Utilities
/Firmware Password Utility.app to your admin computer for later use.

▸ Open the Firmware Password Utility as normal and set the password.

Retrieve the encoded password with nvram:

▸ `sudo nvram security-password`

▸ Copy the encoded text password.

Apply the password and enable firmware protection:

▸ `sudo nvram security-password=encoded_text_password`

▸ `sudo nvram security-mode=command`

To disable firmware protection:

▸ `sudo nvram -d security-mode`

For details, see "System Configuration via Command Line" in
Chapter 6 of *Apple Training Series: Mac OS X Deployment v10.6.*

Modifying Preferences

The best solution is almost always managed preferences.

Use the defaults command to read/write preferences:

▸ When using defaults don't include ".plist" in the preference path.

▸ Preference key = the name of the setting

▸ Preference value = the state of the setting

`defaults read` *preference key*

▸ `defaults read /Library/Preferences
/com.apple.SoftwareUpdate CatalogURL`

`defaults write` *preference key value*

▸ `sudo defaults write /Library/Preferences
/com.apple.SoftwareUpdate CatalogURL
"http://sus.pretendco.com:8088/"`

For details, see "Modifying Preference Configurations" in Chapter 6
of *Apple Training Series: Mac OS X Deployment v10.6.*

Modifying Preferences: ByHost

~/Library/Preferences/ByHost

Preferences are tied to a specific user/computer as determined by a name that includes a computer-specific ID.

You can resolve this name with the `ioreg` command:

▸ `ioreg –rd1 –c IOPlatformExpertDevice | grep –E '(UUID)'`

These items can be renamed with managed preferences or the SIU Apply System Configuration Settings action.

For details, see "Modifying Preference Configurations" in Chapter 6 of *Apple Training Series: Mac OS X Deployment v10.6*.

Postimaging Serialization

Best solution: Obtain multiuser serial numbers.

No built-in or standard method for tracking or managing serialization

Copy file containing license information.

Manually enter serialization information.

Consider licenses management tool (Chapter 7).

For details, see "Understanding Postimaging Client Configuration" in Chapter 6 of *Apple Training Series: Mac OS X Deployment v10.6*.

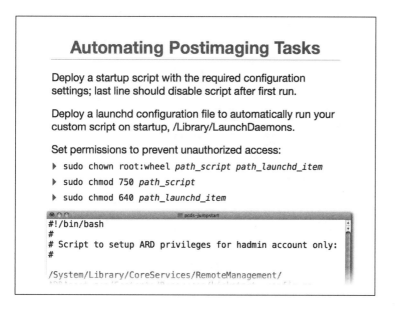

For details, see "Automating Configuration Tasks with launchd" in
Chapter 6 of *Apple Training Series: Mac OS X Deployment v10.6.*

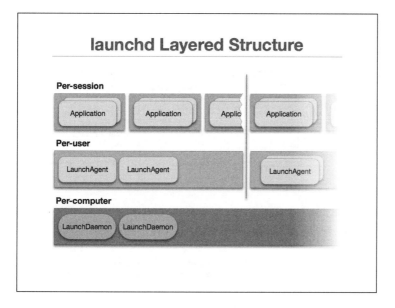

For details, see "Automating Configuration Tasks with launchd" in
Chapter 6 of *Apple Training Series: Mac OS X Deployment v10.6.*

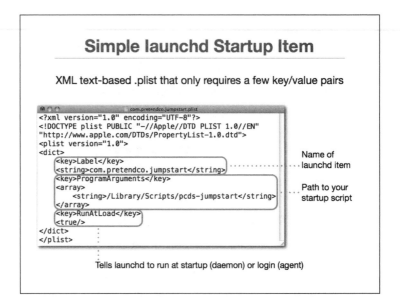

For details, see "Automating Configuration Tasks with launchd" in Chapter 6 of *Apple Training Series: Mac OS X Deployment v10.6*.

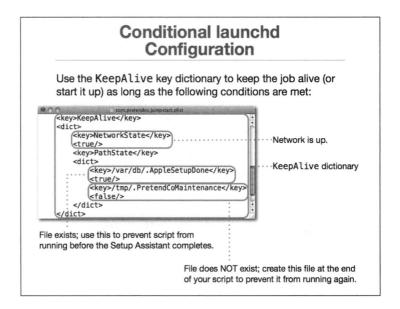

For details, see "Automating Configuration Tasks with launchd" in Chapter 6 of *Apple Training Series: Mac OS X Deployment v10.6*.

Additional launchd Keys

There are too many optional keys to discuss here, but you can read the `launchd.plist` manual page for all the details:

▸ `WorkingDirectory`

  − Specify a directory to change to before running the job.

▸ `EnvironmentVariables`

  − Additional environment variables to be set up before running the job

▸ `UserName`

  − Specifies the user to run the job as

▸ `StartOnMount`

  − Starts the job every time a new file system is mounted

▸ `WatchPaths` or `QueueDirectories`

  − Starts when an item is modified or folder content is added

▸ `StartInterval` or `StartCalendarInterval`

  − Sets a timed interval or a specific calendar interval to run the job

For details, see "Automating Configuration Tasks with launchd" in Chapter 6 of *Apple Training Series: Mac OS X Deployment v10.6*.

launchd Configuration

Per-computer jobs:

▸ /Library/LaunchDaemons/—Third-party daemons

▸ /System/Library/LaunchDaemons/—Apple-supplied daemons

Per-user/session jobs:

▸ ~/Library/LaunchAgents/—Third-party agents for specific user

▸ /Network/Library/LaunchAgents/—Third-party agents for all users

▸ /Library/LaunchAgents/—Third-party agents for all users

▸ /System/Library/LaunchAgents/—Apple-supplied agents

Immediately load/unload laundchd items:

▸ `sudo launchctl load -w path_to_launchd.plist`

▸ `sudo launchctl unload -w path_to_launchd.plist`

For details, see "Automating Configuration Tasks with launchd" in Chapter 6 of *Apple Training Series: Mac OS X Deployment v10.6*.

Login/Logout Scripts

LoginHook/LogoutHook

▸ For all users, execute a script at user login or logout.

▸ Logout-based execution is not possible with `launchd`.

▸ `sudo defaults write com.apple.loginwindow LoginHook` *script_path*

▸ `sodo defaults write com.apple.loginwindow LogoutHook` *script_path*

Launch agent .plist files:

▸ Execute scripts at any point the user is logged into the system.

▸ All users stored in /Library/LaunchAgents

▸ User-specific stored in ~/Library/LaunchAgents

For details, see "Automating Configuration Tasks with loginwindow" in Chapter 6 of *Apple Training Series: Mac OS X Deployment v10.6.*

Exercise 6.1.1
Update Client Settings Using ARD

Objective

- Use Apple Remote Desktop (ARD) to set various client settings, including the steps necessary to bind to an Open Directory server

In this exercise you will remotely configure your Client computer to use your Server computer as a time server. Then you will remotely set computer-specific network settings before binding the computer to your server's directory service. Finally, you will remotely install and serialize Apple QuickTime Pro software.

Change Network Time Settings Using ARD

When binding to a Directory Server, authentication mechanisms are used that rely on timestamps. In order to prevent errors that may occur due to a client and a server being outside of a time tolerance, it's a good idea to use a common time server.

You will use ARD's Send UNIX Command to update the network time settings of your Client computer. First, you will need to verify that the Network Time Protocol (NTP) is running on your server.

1   On your Server computer, open Server Admin and select your Server computer.

2   Under Settings > General, verify that Network Time Server (NTP) is enabled.

    If it is not, select it and click Save.

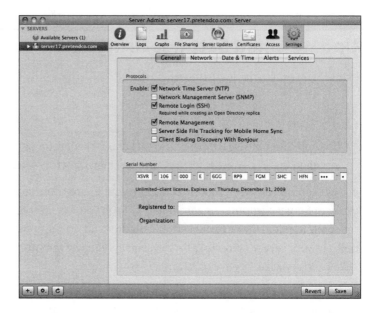

3   Select the Date and Time tab and set the time server to
    127.127.1.0.

> **Note** You may need to wait for 15 minutes or so for the ntpd
> daemon to start serving clock synchronization requests.

4   Open Remote Desktop, select the lab1 computer list, and select
    your Client computer.

5   Choose Manage > Send UNIX Command and type the following
    (with each command on one line and replacing *n* with your
    student number):

    ```
    systemsetup -setnetworktimeserver servern.\
    pretendco.com
    ```

    ```
    systemsetup -setusingnetworktime on
    ```

6   Select to send as user root and then click Send.

You have now set your Client computer to synchronize its clock with your server. Though it's used here as an example of remote client configuration, this setting could easily be incorporated into your system image.

Change Computer Name Using ARD

Before binding your Client computer to the Directory Server, you will update the computer name for easy identification. Setting unique computer names is a necessity for any large deployment and is required for authenticated directory binding.

The Remote Desktop application includes a graphical Rename Computer task. In this case, however, you will use the equivalent UNIX command as this will be included in a script to be used in a later exercise.

1   Select your client machine in the lab1 computer list.

2   Choose Manage > Send UNIX Command and type the following (where *n* is your student number):

```
systemsetup -setcomputername "PretendCo Client n"
```

3   Select to send as user root and then click Send.

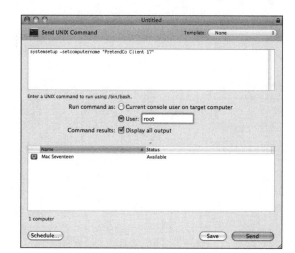

You have now set your Client computer's computer name.

To set your computer's Bonjour name, use a similar Send UNIX command action with scutil.

Change Network TCP/IP Settings Using ARD

There remains one more change before you can bind the Client computer: You will update network preferences on your Client computer to use a static IP address instead of DHCP. As you learned in Chapter 5, DHCP is required to deploy using NetBoot, but many environments require static addressing for administrative purposes. This is not a requirement for using a directory server, but it does make it easier to locate specific client computers on the network.

1   Select your client machine in the lab1 computer list again.

2   Choose Manage > Send UNIX Command and type the following:

    networksetup -listnetworkserviceorder

3   Select to send as user root and then click Send.

    ARD reports the order of network services active for your Client computer.

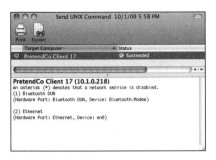

Note the name of the built-in Ethernet ("Ethernet," en0).

4 Send another UNIX command to the same computer to set a
   static IP address, DNS server, and search domain for the built-in
   Ethernet (replacing *n* with your student number):

```
networksetup -setmanual "Ethernet" 10.1.n.2 \
255.255.0.0 10.1.0.1
```

```
networksetup -setdnsservers "Ethernet" 10.1.0.1
```

```
networksetup -setsearchdomains "Ethernet" \
pretendco.com
```

5 Select to send as user root and then click Send.

6 On your client machine, log in as cadmin and use System
   Preferences to see the changes to the network settings,
   computer name, and time server settings.

Now that you've set up the manual IP settings and time server information, you're ready to bind the Client computer to your server.

Bind Your Client to Your Directory Server Using ARD

You will now bind your Client computer to your server's directory service.

1 In the Remote Desktop lab1 computer list, select your Client computer again.

2 Choose Manage > Send UNIX Command and type the following to make sure LDAP is active on your Client computer (all on one line):

```
defaults write /Library/Preferences/\
DirectoryService/DirectoryService LDAPv3 Active
```

3 Send the command as user root.

4 Send another UNIX command to restart the DirectoryService process on your Client computer:

```
killall DirectoryService
```

5 Send the command as user root.

6 Send another UNIX command to add the new LDAP entry to directory services on your client machine (replace *n* with your student number):

```
dsconfigldap -v -a servern.pretendco.com
```

7 Send as user root.

A new LDAP entry should now be present in Directory Utility on the Client computer.

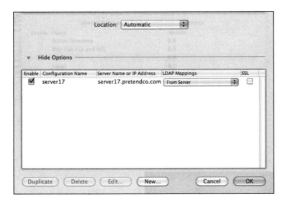

8   Set the Search Path for LDAP Authentication (with each command on a separate line and *n* as your student number):

```
dscl /Search -create / SearchPolicy CSPSearchPath
```

```
dscl /Search -append / CSPSearchPath /LDAPv3/\
servern.pretendco.com
```

9   Send as user root.

Check your Client computer's directory services search policy, again by looking in Directory Utility.

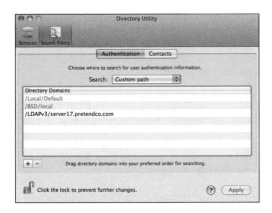

10 On your client machine, log out of the cadmin account and log in as a network user (that is, morty; password: morty) to test the binding to your server.

11 Once tested, log out and back in as cadmin.

Send an Application and Serial Number to a Limited Number of Client Computers

In some cases you may want to limit a customization to a specific set of computers. In this exercise you have one additional license key for QuickTime Player 7 that you will send out to your Client computer.

1 On your Server computer, double-click the com.apple. QuickTime.plist file that resides in the Student Materials/ Chapter6 folder.

   Notice how the serial number is displayed and can be edited.

   You may need to expand a couple of disclosure triangles in order to view the serial number.

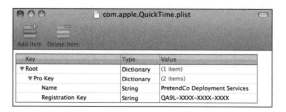

2 Close the plist file.

3 Open Remote Desktop and select your Client computer from the lab1 computer list.

4 Choose Manage > Install Packages.

5 Drag the QuickTimePlayer7.pkg from the Student Materials/ Chapter6 folder into the Install Packages window.

6 Click Install.

   Next, you will send the license key.

7 With your Client computer still selected, choose Manage > Copy Items.

8 Drag the com.apple.QuickTime.plist file from the Student Materials/Chapter6 folder into the Copy Items window.

9   Select "Place items in" and "Specify full path" and then enter:

    `/Library/Preferences`

10 Click OK and select to rename the item if it already exists.

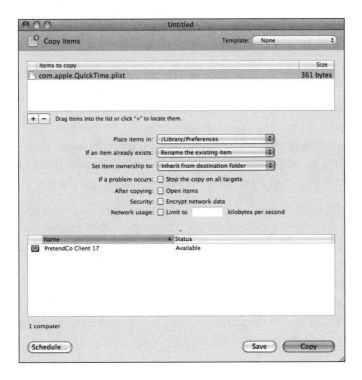

11 Click Copy to copy the license file to the Client computer.

12 On your Client computer, open QuickTime Player 7 (located in /Applications/Utilities).

13 From the Application menu, choose Registration to see the new registration information you just sent over.

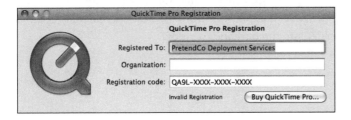

Exercise 6.1.2

Configure Automated Scripts

Objective

- Configure a `launchd` daemon to run once at first boot to customize computer settings

When you deploy system images to new computers, you can include most settings and customizations in the deployed system image. There are some settings (such as computer name) that should be set postimaging, and some settings (such as those for ARD 3) that can be set during a client machine's first startup.

In this exercise you will examine a custom `launchd` daemon to run once during a computer's first boot. The `launchd` daemon in this exercise creates and configures ARD settings for the hadmin account. Though we are enabling this `launchd` daemon after deployment, it certainly could be included as part of your system image. Deploying this `launchd` daemon as an installation package makes it easy for you to go back and incorporate it into your modular system image workflow.

Set a Launch Daemon to Run at First Startup

You will copy an existing Launch Daemon to your Client computer and configure it to run when the Client computer first boots.

1 Open Remote Desktop on your Server computer and select your Client computer from the lab1 computer list.

2 Choose Manage > Install Packages and drag the jumpstart. pkg installation package from the Student Materials/Chapter6 folder into the packages window.

3   Click Install to install the package on your Client computer.

The jumpstart.pkg package installs updated versions
/Library/Scripts/pcds-startup and /Library/LaunchDaemons/
com.pretendco.startup.plist (from Chapter 4) onto the client
machine.

The updated version of pcds-startup includes many of the
ARD UNIX commands you have just sent—with conditional
logic that makes sure they are only run once on first boot.

Both payload files are located in the Student Materials/
Chapter6 folder.

4   On your Server computer, right-click on Student Materials/
Chapter6/pcds-startup and choose Open With > TextWrangler
to see what it will do when executed.

5   Close the file when done.

6   Restart your Client computer to run your custom launchd daemon.

7   Login as cadmin.

Question 1 *What new hidden file resides in the /Users folder?*

Configure LogoutHook Script (optional)

You will configure a LogoutHook to run an existing script every
time a user logs out of the Client computer. You can also use this
technique to set up a LogoutHook script that runs every time a
user logs in to your client machine. This can also be incorporated
into your system image.

1   Open Remote Desktop on your Server computer and select
your client machine from the lab1 computer list.

2   Choose Manage > Copy Items.

3   Use ARD's Copy Items to copy the Student Materials/Chapter6/ logouthook script to the /Library/Scripts folder on your Client computer.

4   Use Send UNIX Command in ARD to change the ownership of the LogoutHook script:

```
chown root:admin /Library/Scripts/logouthook
```

5   Send command as user root.

6   Send another UNIX command to your Client computer to activate the LogoutHook with the defaults command:

```
defaults write com.apple.loginwindow \
LogoutHook /Library/Scripts/logouthook
```

7   Send command as user root.

To test the effectiveness of this LogoutHook, all you need to do is check the contents of ~/Library/Caches before and after logging out and back in again.

8   On your client machine, use Terminal to open the folder ~/Library/Caches.

9   Note the existence of the cache files.

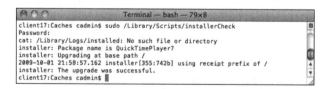

10 Log out of your Client computer and log back in as cadmin.

11 Use Terminal one more time to check the contents of ~/Library/Caches.

Without the LogoutHook in place, you will have Cache files still populating your home folder ~/Library/Caches.

Exercise 6.1.3
Install Packages Automatically From a Server

Objective

- Set up a script to run at system startup that will copy new packages from an Apple Filing Protocol (AFP) server and install them on a Client computer

In previous exercises you have relied heavily upon ARD to deliver customizations and files to Client computers. Alternatively you can set a startup task on the Client computers to "phone in" to a server to pick up and run available updates.

This script will serve as a precursor to the software update exercises in Chapter 7; here you will create a mechanism to use your AFP server to provide installers that will be automatically installed on your client machine at startup. In this case you need to restart the computer to initiate the update process; in Chapter 7 you will learn how to set this task on a repeating schedule.

Create an Automated Download and Installation Mechanism

You will customize a template script that will be used to download available updates from your server and install them on your Client computer.

1 On your Server computer, use TextWrangler (not TextEdit) to edit the installerCheck file located in the Student Materials/Chapter6 folder. As you did with a similar script in Chapter 4, replace *n* with your student number in the following line:

snum=*n*

For example, if your student number is 17, you would edit the line to read:

snum=17

> **Note** Do not use TextEdit: It adds a .txt extension to the file that will cause the installation mechanism to fail.

2   Save your change.

3   Open Remote Desktop and select your Client computer from the lab1 computer list.

4   Use the Copy Items feature in ARD to copy the installerCheck script from the Student Materials/Chapter6 to the /Library/ Scripts folder on your Client computer.

Next you will set up the installerCheck script to run every time the computer starts up.

5   Use Copy Items in ARD again, this time to copy com.pretendco. installerCheck.plist from the Student Materials/Chapter6 folder to the /Library/LaunchDaemons folder on your Client computer.

6   Send a UNIX command to change the ownership and permissions of the installerCheck script:

```
chown root:admin /Library/Scripts/installerCheck

chmod a+x /Library/Scripts/installerCheck
```

7   Send as user root.

The launchd daemon on your Client computer will run the installerCheck script once every time your Client computer starts up.

Test-Run the Automatic Download and Installation Mechanism

Instead of waiting until the next startup to have this script run, you will run it manually to install a test package now.

1   On your server, copy the Rosetta installation package from the Student Materials/Chapter6 folder to your Deployment Library *n*/autoinstall share point.

Rosetta is an optional install from the Mac OS X Install DVD that we elected not to distribute as part of the core image.

Now you will allow Client computers to download this application and install it. If there are no other installation packages (besides jumpstart.pkg) in the Student Materials/Chapter6 folder, please inform your instructor. You will be directed to an alternative installation package for use with this exercise.

2   Open Terminal on your client and run the installerCheck manually at the command line:

`sudo /Library/Scripts/installerCheck`

The script will report back any installations it is performing.

> **Note** If the script reports an error "-5023," stop and start AFP services on your server and try running the script again.

`client17:Desktop hadmin$ sudo /Library/Scripts/ installerCheck`

`installer: Package name is Rosetta`

`installer: Upgrading at base path /`

`2009-10-06 19:03:30.554 installer[609:752b] using receipt prefix of /`

`installer: The upgrade was successful.`

3   Check the log file created by this script:

`more /Library/Logs/installed`

4   You should see one entry for the new package that you placed on the Deployment Library share point.

5   Run the script again using the command in Step 2.

Question 2 Did the same installation package get installed again?

6.2 Postimaging Server Configuration

Even more so than client systems, server systems also require unique configurations. Even in situations where servers are very similar, such as computational clusters or servers set up for load balancing or failover, unique serialization and network configuration are still necessary. As such, Mac OS X Server includes an automatic server setup technology that can be used to completely automate the initial required server settings. Here you will learn how to take advantage of this system to automatically configure a fresh install of Mac OS X Server.

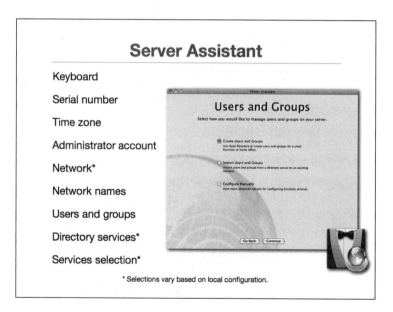

For details, see "Understanding Automatic Server Setup" in Chapter 6 of *Apple Training Series: Mac OS X Deployment v10.6.*

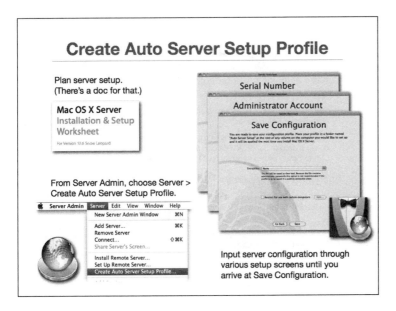

For details, see "Using Automatic Server Setup" in Chapter 6 of
Apple Training Series: Mac OS X Deployment v10.6.

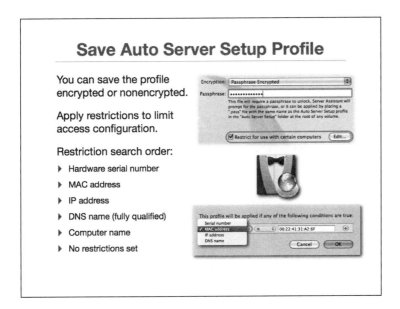

For details, see "Using Automatic Server Setup" in Chapter 6 of
Apple Training Series: Mac OS X Deployment v10.6.

Deploy Auto Server Setup

Server Assistant scans for auto
server setup profiles:

▶ Any mounted volume containing an
   Auto Server Setup folder

▶ Any XML file in these folders with a
   name ending in ".plist" is inspected for
   Server Setup profile information.

Encrypted setup profile:

▶ Manually enter password at Setup
   Assistant screen (ARD or VNC).

▶ Place a TXT file containing the
   password in an Auto Server Setup
   folder with same name as the
   encrypted profile but ending in ".pass."

For details, see "Using Automatic Server Setup" in Chapter 6 of
Apple Training Series: Mac OS X Deployment v10.6.

Exercise 6.2.1
Use the Automatic Server Setup System

Objective

- Set up a Mac OS X Server to get its configuration automatically from a Directory Server after a fresh install

Most, if not all, of the previous exercises have involved deployment of Mac OS X. Here you will focus on one of the many ways you can streamline the setup of Mac OS X Server.

> **Note** If you elected not to complete Exercise 5.2.3, "Create a Server NetInstall Image (optional)," follow your instructor's directions for using the Server NetInstall image that is available from your instructor's server.

Use NetInstall to Reinstall Mac OS X Server

You will reinstall server software onto a new partition on your Server computer and then use an AutoServerSetup.plist file to configure initial settings.

Because a reinstall will wipe out your existing server configuration, you'll partition your Server computer's hard drive to make room for this fresh install and thereby save your original server setup for use in the remaining exercises.

Use Server Admin and Setup Assistant to Save Your Configuration Settings

1   On the Server computer, log in as ladmin and open Server Admin.

2   Choose Server > Create Auto Server Setup Profile.

    Server Assistant opens to the keyboard selection screen.

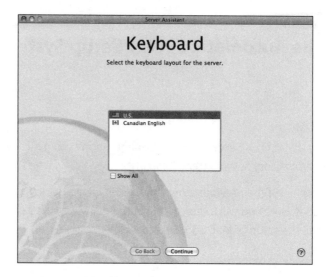

3   Click Continue and use the following information as you progress
    through Server Assistant (replacing *n* with your student number):

- Keyboard: US

- Serial Number: Ask your instructor

- Registered to: PretendCo

- Organization: Training

- Time Zone: Ask your instructor

- Account Name: Local Administrator

- Short Name: ladmin

- Password: ladmin

- Verify: ladmin

- Enable Remote Management and SSH (the default)

- Network Interfaces: Add the default "Ethernet," "en0" with
  your Server's MAC address (available in System Preferences
  or by using ifconfig in Terminal).

- Configure IPv4: Manually

- IP Address: 10.1.*n*.1

- Subnet Mask: 255.255.0.0

- Router: 10.1.0.1

- DNS Servers: 10.1.0.1

- Search Domains: pretendco.com

- IPv6: Switch off

- Primary DNS Name: server$n$.pretendco.com

- Computer Name: server$n$

- Users and Groups: Configure Manually

- Connected to a Directory Server: no

- Directory Services: do not set up an Open Directory master

- Encryption: none

- Restrict for use with certain computers: edit

4   Change the condition to MAC Address and enter your server's
    MAC address.

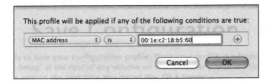

5   Click OK.

6   Click Save and save the configuration file as AutoServerSetup$n$.
    plist to your desktop for now.

7   Click Start Over and quit Server Assistant.

8   In the Finder, create a new folder called Auto Server Setup in
    the root of your server's current boot volume.

9   Copy (Option-drag) the configuration file (AutoServerSetup$n$.
    plist) you just created from the desktop and into the /Auto
    Server Setup folder.

Use Property List Editor to View and Edit the Configuration File

Use Property List Editor to view the contents of the configuration file:

1   Double-click the AutoServerSetup*n*.plist file in the /Auto Server Setup folder.

    Property List Editor will open and allow you to view the contents of the configuration file.

2   View the entry in the XML of this plist file for applicableServersPredicate—it lists your Server's MAC address.

3   Expand the entries for config and then adminUser.

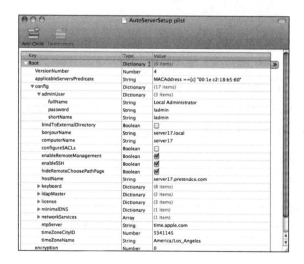

Notice that in this unencrypted copy of the server setup file, the adminUser's password is clearly readable.

4   Edit the entries for maximumOSVersion and minimumOSVersion to reflect the version of Mac OS X Server used in your NetInstall image from Exercise 5.2.3.

You may obtain this information from your instructor if using the instructor's NetInstall image for Mac OS X Server.

5   Save and close your setup file.

NetInstall Mac OS X Server

Your instructor may elect to provide the NetInstall image, used for this part of the exercise, from the classroom server.

Alternatively, if you completed Exercise 5.2.3, your server may be chosen to provide the NetInstall image for other servers in the classroom. If so, you need only perform the first few steps of this exercise—enabling the Server NetInstall image with Server Admin.

Conversely, if you are going to NetInstall your server, skip past the first steps for enabling the Server NetInstall image and start at the point where you will create a second partition on your server's hard drive with Disk Utility.

1   Open Server Admin on the Server computer that will supply the NetInstall image.

2   Select the NetBoot service and then select the checkbox to enable the image for Server NetInstall *n* that you created earlier (where *n* is your student number).

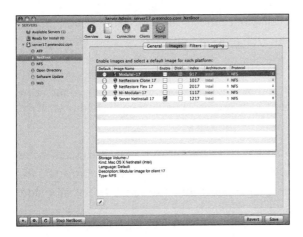

3   Click Save.

> **Note** Your instructor may provide the Server NetInstall image for you.

4   On the server that will receive the NetInstall image, open Disk Utility and add another partition called Server2.

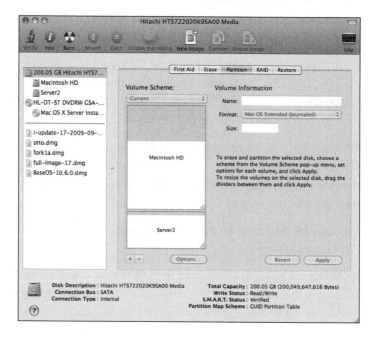

5   Close Disk Utility once the partition has been created and then open System Preferences.

> **Note** The above Disk Utility operation could have also been completed while you were booted from the NetInstall image.

6   Click Startup Disk, select the Server NetInstall *n* image (where *n* is the student number for the student server providing the NetInstall image) or select your instructor's NetInstall image, and click Restart.

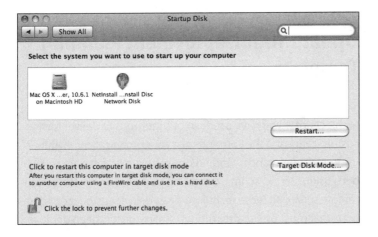

7   Click Restart again, and your Server computer will start up from the NetInstall image.

8   Once your Server computer starts up from the NetInstall image, proceed through the installer steps to initiate installation of Mac OS X Server on the Server2 partition.

9   Click Restart when prompted.

Upon restart, the Server computer that received the fresh copy of Mac OS X Server will pull the configuration settings that were saved on your server's initial boot partition and configure itself.

Once your server is reconfigured, it will reboot and present you with the familiar login window.

10 Log in and reboot from the original partition.

Exercise 6.2.2

Update Your Deployment Planning Template

In this chapter you have used various methods to deliver further customizations to the computers in your organization. Whether using ARD commands, sending out software or software serial numbers, using startup scripts, or getting packages and settings from a remote server, all these techniques can deliver custom configurations that must be set after the system image has been deployed.

Computer names and software serial numbers are often computer-specific and do not lend themselves well to being included in your main operating system image. However, if you intend to deploy these postimaging configurations using automated scripting mechanisms that run when your new system is first booted, then you can include those items as part of your system image. Furthermore, you can easily integrate these items into your modular system image workflow by deploying them inside an installer package.

Now it's time to update your template to see which of the various methods demonstrated lend themselves to your particular situation:

- Send UNIX commands via ARD for various computer settings (name, time, and so on)

- Copy files via ARD for unique preference files (including serialization of software)

- Use startup scripts such as `launchd` daemons

- Store server configuration information in a text file

When you fill out your template, please remember to include the rationale for using these forms of deployment.

7

System Maintenance

7.1   System Maintenance

Exercise 7.1.1   Use ARD to Monitor Systems
Exercise 7.1.2   Integrating ARD with Directory Services

7.2   Using Software Update Server and Maintenance Tasks

Exercise 7.2.1   Set Up Software Update Server
Exercise 7.2.2   Configure Clients to Use Software Update Server
Exercise 7.2.3   Configure Periodic Maintenance Tasks
Exercise 7.2.4   Update Your Deployment Planning Template

7.1 System Maintenance

The pace of computer technology is relentless, especially when it comes to software. It's not uncommon for Apple to release an average of one software update every week. Add to that updates to third-party software and new additional software, and it can be a daunting task just to keep your deployed systems maintained. Along with new software, additional configuration changes often need to be deployed as well. Finally, there is the issue of monitoring changes to deployed systems to ensure their consistency. All these system maintenance tasks are necessary to keep your deployed systems running smoothly.

System Maintenance Concepts

Remote administration and system monitoring

Asset and license management

Software additions and maintenance

For details, see "Understanding System Maintenance Concepts" in Chapter 7 of *Apple Training Series: Mac OS X Deployment v10.6*.

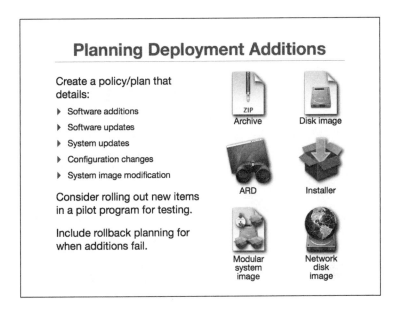

For details, see "Understanding System Maintenance Concepts" in Chapter 7 of *Apple Training Series: Mac OS X Deployment v10.6.*

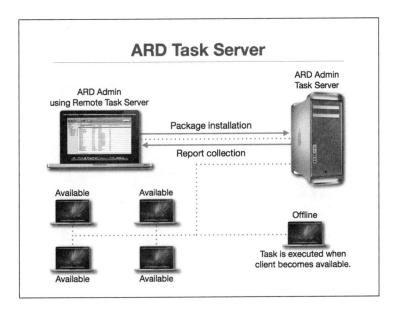

For details, see "Using an ARD Task Server" in Chapter 7 of *Apple Training Series: Mac OS X Deployment v10.6.*

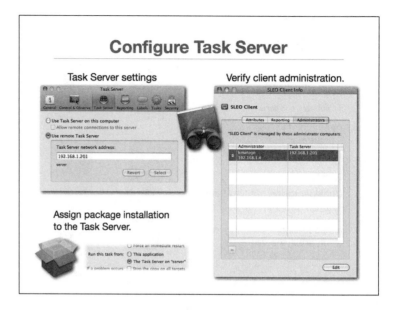

For details, see "Using an ARD Task Server" in Chapter 7 of
Apple Training Series: Mac OS X Deployment v10.6.

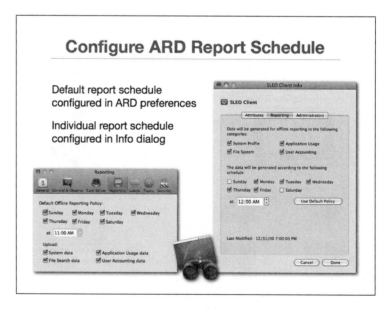

For details, see "Using ARD to Create Reports" in Chapter 7 of
Apple Training Series: Mac OS X Deployment v10.6.

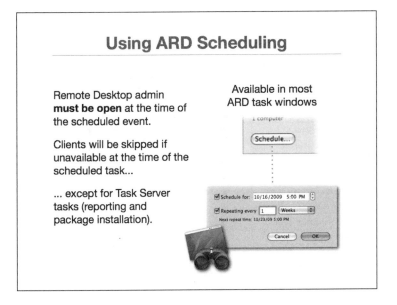

For details, see "Using ARD to Schedule Tasks" in Chapter 7 of
Apple Training Series: Mac OS X Deployment v10.6.

For details, see "Configuring ARD Directory Service Integration" in
Chapter 7 of *Apple Training Series: Mac OS X Deployment v10.6.*

ARD Privilege Keys

Use these ARD management privileges keys as group names or in custom managed preference settings:

Management Privilege	ard_admin	ard_reports	ard_manage	ard_interact
Generate reports	●	●	●	
Open and quit applications	●		●	
Change settings	●		●	
Copy items	●		●	
Delete and replace items	●		●	
Send messages	●		●	●
Restart and shut down	●		●	
Control	●			●
Observe	●			●
Show being observed	●			●

For details, see "Configuring ARD Directory Service Integration" in Chapter 7 of *Apple Training Series: Mac OS X Deployment v10.6.*

Exercise 7.1.1
Use ARD to Monitor Systems

Objective

- Use ARD to generate Usage and Application reports for your Client computer

In this class you have been using a Task Server to upload and track application usage and user history information. You can make use of this information with the Remote Desktop reports feature, some of which you used in Chapter 1.

Run ARD Application Report for Your Client Computer

Use ARD to run an application usage report based on data from your Client computer.

1   On your Server computer, log in as ladmin and open Remote Desktop.

2   Select your Client computer from the lab1 computer list and choose Report > Application Usage from the menu bar.

3   Click Generate Report.

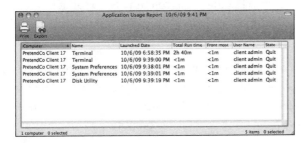

4   View the report and export it to your desktop as "Final App Report *n*" (where *n* is your student number).

If you do not see (m)any results, increase the date range for your report.

This report shows all the applications that have been used on your Client computer. Since most of the activity on your Client computer involved system settings, you should see System Preferences and Installer listed as the most frequently used applications.

Running this report on a deployed Client computer that is undergoing normal use should generate a report that contains more user-oriented application usage.

Run ARD User History Report for Your Client Computer

Use ARD to run a user history report based on data from your client.

1   On your server, in Remote Desktop select your Client computer from the lab1 computer list.

2   Choose Report > User History from the menu bar.

3   Click Generate Report.

4   View the report, click the Login column title to sort it by ascending login time, and then export it to your desktop as "Final User Report *n*" (where *n* is your student number).

This report shows which users have logged in and out of your Client computer. Running this report on a deployed Client computer that is used by more than one user helps track which users (local and network) have been using your Client computer and for how long.

> **Warning!** If you are unable to generate reports from your Client computer, check that it is configured with ARD client software that is compatible with your Task Server and your server installs of ARD.

Exercise 7.1.2
Integrating ARD with Directory Services

Objective

- Use ARD and Directory Service accounts to manage your Client computer

So far, you have been relying on user accounts and Remote Management settings on the Client computer in order for control to be passed to your ARD administration workstation.

In this exercise you will make use of Managed Preferences and centralized user accounts to provide the same functionality.

Creating Network ARD Administrator Accounts

Use Workgroup Manager to create groups in your LDAP database that you will assign users for ARD control on your Client computer.

1 On your Server computer, log in as ladmin and open Workgroup Manager.

2 Click the Accounts icon in the toolbar and click Groups.

3 Create four new groups in your shared domain using the following information:

Long Name	Short Name
ard_admin	ard_admin
ard_reports	ard_reports
ard_interact	ard_interact
ard_manage	ard_manage

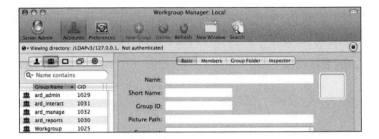

4   Next make sure the user morty is a member of the ard_admin group and click Save.

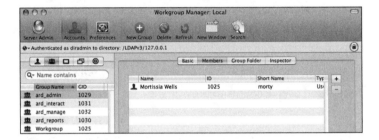

Change Client Settings to Allow Directory Authentication

Use ARD to change client settings to allow directory users to control your Client computer.

1   On your Server computer, open ARD and chose Manage > Change Client Settings.

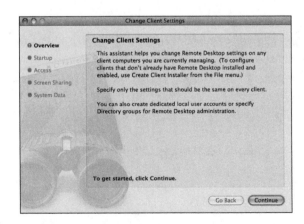

2   At the initial screen, click Continue.

3   At the Starting Remote Desktop screen, disable menu visibility and click Continue.

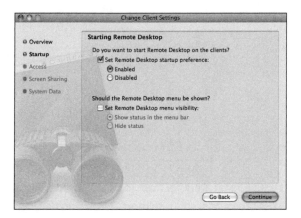

4   At the User Accounts screen, click Continue.

5   At the Incoming Access screen, enable directory-based administration and click Continue.

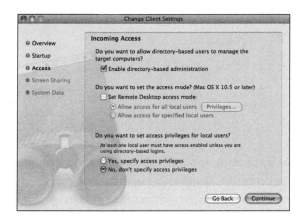

6   At the Screen Sharing Options and System Data screens, click Continue.

7   Click Change to send these changes to your Client computer.

8 Next select your Client computer from the All Computers list and change the user account settings to morty (replacing hadmin).

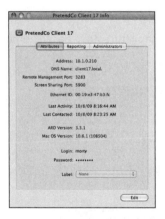

9 Lastly, use ARD to control your Client computer with the network account: morty. You are now able to control your Client computer with user accounts that are centrally managed.

> **Note** If you want to use the kickstart command to enable directory authentication, these are the options:
>
> ```
> kickstart -configure -clientopts -setdirlogins
> -dirlogins yes
> ```
>
> ```
> kickstart -configure -access -on -restart -agent
> ```

Using Software Update Server and Maintenance Tasks

7.2

Two of the mechanisms available to system administrators are the Software Update Server and periodic maintenance scripts. While the former is not configured on a new server install, the latter maintenance scripts are. In this lesson you will look at how to set up and customize Software Update Server to provide a cascading software update service and then make use of the preexisting periodic task functions to run your own maintenance scripts.

Periodic Maintenance

periodic daily
▸ Runs at 3:15 a.m.
▸ Executes scripts in /etc/periodic/daily/

periodic weekly
▸ Runs every Saturday at 3:15 a.m.
▸ Executes scripts in /etc/periodic/weekly/

periodic monthly
▸ Runs every first day of the month at 5:30 a.m.
▸ Executes scripts in /etc/periodic/monthly/

```
$ ls -c1 /etc/periodic/
daily/
100.clean-logs
110.clean-tmps
130.clean-msgs
430.status-rwho
500.daily
600.daily.server
601.daily.server.krb5kdc
700.daily.server.cyrus
```

For details, see "Automating System Maintenance Scripts" in Chapter 7 of *Apple Training Series: Mac OS X Deployment v10.6*.

Add Your Own Periodic Scripts

Move your script into the right folder:

▸ /etc/periodic/daily/, /etc/periodic/weekly/, or /etc/periodic/monthly/

Add a number to beginning of name to set the order.

Set the appropriate permissions for the script:

▸ `sudo chown root:wheel path_to_script`

▸ `sudo chmod 550 path_to_script`

Optionally, modify the periodic schedule (launchd):

▸ /System/Library/LaunchDaemons/com.apple.periodic-daily.plist

▸ /System/Library/LaunchDaemons/com.apple.periodic-weekly.plist

▸ /System/Library/LaunchDaemons/com.apple.periodic-monthly.plist

For details, see "Automating System Maintenance Scripts" in Chapter 7 of *Apple Training Series: Mac OS X Deployment v10.6.*

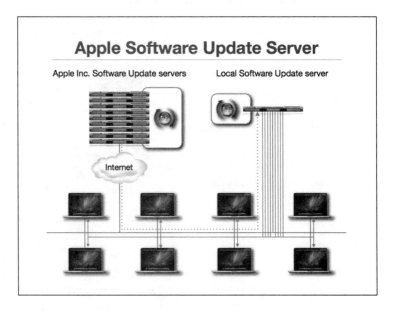

Apple Software Update Server

Apple Inc. Software Update servers   Local Software Update server

Internet

For details, see "Configuring Apple Software Update Service" in Chapter 7 of *Apple Training Series: Mac OS X Deployment v10.6.*

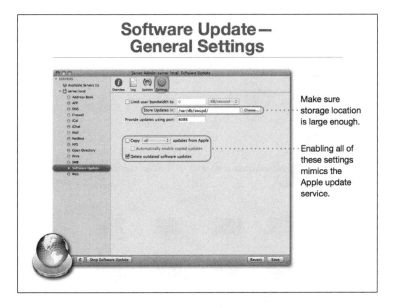

For details, see "Configuring Apple Software Update Service" in Chapter 7 of *Apple Training Series: Mac OS X Deployment v10.6.*

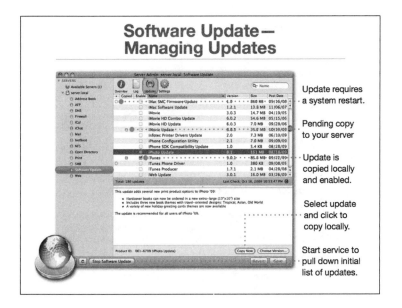

For details, see "Configuring Apple Software Update Service" in Chapter 7 of *Apple Training Series: Mac OS X Deployment v10.6.*

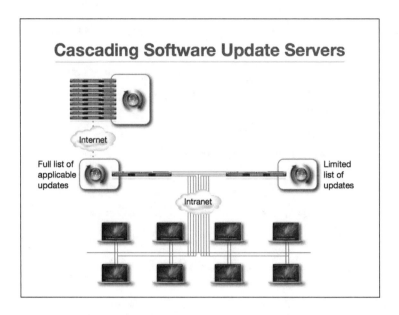

For details, see "Using Cascading Software Update Servers" in
Chapter 7 of *Apple Training Series: Mac OS X Deployment v10.6.*

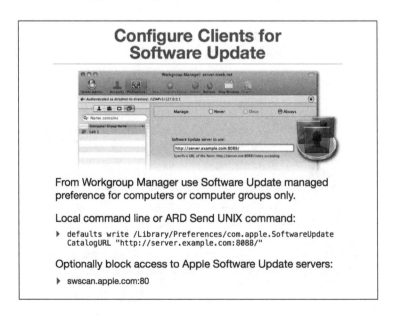

For details, see "Configuring Clients for Your Software Update Service"
in Chapter 7 of *Apple Training Series: Mac OS X Deployment v10.6.*

Manually Initiate Software Update

Automatic software update is a per-user preference, thus disabling it requires one of the following techniques:

▸ Incorporate command string "`softwareupdate --schedule off`" into a launch agent or login hook script.

▸ Use managed preferences via Workgroup Manager to import the ByHost preference, ~/Library/Preferences/ByHost/com.apple.scheduler.*UUID*.plist.

Install all available Apple software updates:

▸ `sudo softwareupdate --install --all`

Note that many Apple system updates require a system restart.

For details, see "Configuring Clients for Your Software Update Service" in Chapter 7 of *Apple Training Series: Mac OS X Deployment v10.6.*

Troubleshooting Software Update

Ensure appropriate services are running:

▸ `swupd-syncd`—Downloads list and updates (rarely running)

▸ `httpd-1.3`—Shares downloaded updates to network

Ensure proper packages are downloaded and enabled:

▸ Default location is /var/db/swupd/html/.

▸ Enabled packages match clients

Test network issues:

▸ DNS and host name configuration

▸ Appropriate TCP ports open—defaults are 80 and 8088

Ensure server can connect to "upstream" update servers.

Ensure client preference points to correct URL.

For details, see "Troubleshooting the Software Update Service" in Chapter 7 of *Apple Training Series: Mac OS X Deployment v10.6.*

Third-Party Tools:
Remote Administration

Any standard VNC client can remotely monitor and control a Mac, enabled via screen sharing or remote management prefs.

The following are commercial remote monitoring and administration tolls that provide cross-platform support:

LanSchool

Timbuktu Pro

NetSupport Manager

For details, see "Third-Party System Maintenance Tools" in Chapter 7 of *Apple Training Series: Mac OS X Deployment v10.6.*

Third-Party Tools:
Asset and License Management

Alteris

**FileWave
Asset Trustee**

Recon Suite

**KeyAuditor &
KeyServer**

Only K2's KeyServer provides third-party software license enforcement for the Mac.

For details, see "Third-Party System Maintenance Tools" in Chapter 7 of *Apple Training Series: Mac OS X Deployment v10.6.*

Third-Party Tools:
Software Additions and Maintenance

Each one of these third-party tools provides a unique
approach to software management:

Deep Freeze
Maintains consistent software

 Puppet

Puppet
System management language (FOSS)

Radmind
Package management and deployment (FOSS)

For details, see "Third-Party System Maintenance Tools" in
Chapter 7 of *Apple Training Series: Mac OS X Deployment v10.6.*

Third-Party Tools:
System Management Suites

Commercial suites that provide packaging, imaging,
maintenance, inventory, etc., along with customer support:

KACE
Systems Management. Done.

LANrev

**Casper Suite
by JAMF**

KACE

LANrev

 filewave

 LANDesk
An Avocent Company

FileWave

LANDesk

For details, see "Third-Party System Maintenance Tools" in
Chapter 7 of *Apple Training Series: Mac OS X Deployment v10.6.*

Exercise 7.2.1
Set Up Software Update Server

Objective

- Configure and start the Software Update service (SUS) on your server

In this exercise you will configure your Server computer to reshare software updates provided by Apple. You'll configure the Software Update preferences to point your server to the main classroom server to form a cascading server arrangement. For expediency reasons mainserver provides only a small number of updates.

Use the Classroom Server as an SUS for Your Server

You will configure your Server computer to use the classroom server, mainserver, as a source for software updates and ensure that your server can access those updates.

1 On your Server computer, open the hidden folder /etc/swupd and edit the /etc/swupd/swupd.plist file using TextWrangler.

2 Find the value for this key:

`<key>metaIndexURL</key>`

It should read something like this:

`<string>http://swscan.apple.com/content/meta/mirror-config-1.plist</string>`

This is the URL for the catalog of updates provided by Apple.

3 Change the value to (all on one line):

`<string>http://mainserver.pretendco.com:8088/catalogs.sucatalog</string>`

This is the URL for the update catalog on the main classroom server.

4   Save the file.

The next step is to start the service.

Start the Software Update Service

You will start the Software Update service on your Server computer.

1   On your Server computer, open Server Admin and select the Software Update service.

2   Click the Settings icon in the toolbar.

3   Leave the default port as 8088.

4   Select "Copy all updates from Apple."

5   Select "Automatically enable copied updates."

6   Select "Delete outdated software updates."

7   Click Save and start the service.

Click Updates to see which updates are available for your Server computer to share out to your Client computers.

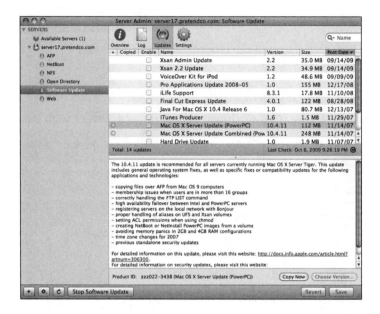

You are now ready to point your Client computers to your functioning Software Update server.

Exercise 7.2.2
Configure Clients to Use Software Update Server

Objective

- Use Workgroup Manager and/or Remote Desktop to set software update settings on the Client computer

For Client computers to use your Software Update server instead of Apple's, you will need to change their configuration.

There are two ways you can tell a Client computer that it should use your Software Update server: by setting managed client settings within Workgroup Manager or by sending a UNIX command to set a default on your Client computer.

Set Software Update Server Managed Client Settings

You will set computer-specific Managed Client settings with Workgroup Manager.

1   On your Server computer, open Workgroup Manager and click the Computer Groups tab.

2   Authenticate into your server's own LDAP domain (127.0.0.1) as diradmin (password: diradmin).

3   Your Client computer should already be listed in the lab1 computer group. If it is not, add it now.

4   Click Preferences in the toolbar and then click Software Update in the Overview pane.

5 Select Always as the management choice and then add the following URL for the Software Update server to use (where *n* is your student number):

`http://servern.pretendco.com:8088/`

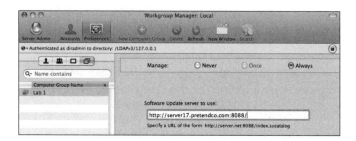

6 Click Apply Now and then click Done.

7 On your Client computer, log out and log back in as cadmin.

Logging out and back in to the Client computer will prompt it to receive the new Managed Preference file.

8 On your Client computer, open /Library/Managed Preferences in the Finder.

A new com.apple.SoftwareUpdate.plist file should be present. If this file is not present, your Client computer has not yet received it. You can trigger your Client computer to fetch new preference settings by restarting the computer.

9 On your Client computer, use the following command in Terminal to read the new software update setting (on one line):

`defaults read /Library/Managed\ Preferences/com.apple. SoftwareUpdate CatalogURL`

The result should report something like this:

`http://server17.pretendco.com:8088/`

10 To test your server's SUS service, open Safari on your Client computer and go to the following URL (where *n* is your student number):

`http://servern.pretendco.com:8088/index.sucatalog`

You should see the XML-formatted list of updates available from your server.

If you do not see a list of updates, please wait while your server downloads them from mainserver.

11 To check that your Client computer will use this Software Update server, log in as morty (password apple), open System Preferences, and run Software Update. Your server's domain name will be in the title bar of the Software Update server window.

> **Note** If you are logged in as an administrator and have disabled Managed Client preferences, you will not get this result.

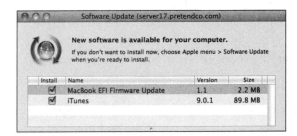

Set Software Update Server with ARD (optional)

Instead of using Managed Client settings, you will set the Software Update server setting using the defaults command.

1 On your Server computer, open Remote Desktop and select your Client computer from the lab1 list.

2 Choose Manage > Send UNIX command and type in the following (all on one line, replacing *n* with your student number):

```
defaults write /Library/Preferences/com.apple.
SoftwareUpdate CatalogURL "http://servern.pretendco.
com:8088/"
```

3 Send as user root.

4 On your Client computer, check the newly created/updated /Library/Preferences/com.apple.SoftwareUpdate.plist file by using this command:

```
defaults read /Library/Preferences/com.apple.
SoftwareUpdate CatalogURL
```

To verify that your Client computer will use this Software Update server, open System Preferences and run Software Update.

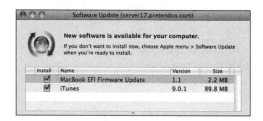

5 Also, you can check to see if the updates are visible to the Client computer by directly viewing the catalog information once again using Safari (replace *n* with your student number):

```
http://servern.pretendco.com:8088/index.sucatalog
```

You have successfully configured your Client computer to use your own Software Update server. In the next exercise you will learn how to check for software updates on a periodic basis.

6 Cancel Software Update; you will not install any updates at this time.

Exercise 7.2.3

Configure Periodic Maintenance Tasks

Objective

- Configure task(s) to run periodically care of `launchd`

In the previous exercise and in Chapter 6, you created actions that check your server for installation packages or approved software updates.

In this exercise you will set up those tasks to run periodically.

Create a Weekly Periodic Task

You will set up a periodic task that runs `softwareupdate` on a weekly basis. This task will also check a server share point for additional installation packages.

1   On your Server computer, use TextWrangler to open the 400. pcds-tasks script from Student Materials/Chapter7.

2   This script runs both /usr/sbin/softwareupate and the installer-Check script you copied into /Library/Scripts in Exercise 6.1.3.

3   Close the script after you have finished reviewing it.

4   Open Remote Desktop and select your Client computer from the lab1 computer list.

5   Use Copy Items in ARD 3 to copy the 400.pcds-tasks script from the Student Materials/Chapter7 folder to the /etc/periodic/ weekly folder on your Client computer.

6   To set the ownership and permissions of the script, send these UNIX commands with ARD:

```
chown root:wheel /etc/periodic/weekly/400.pcds-tasks
chmod ug+x /etc/periodic/weekly/400.pcds-tasks
```

7   Send as user root.

This script will now run once a week.

The scripts inside the /etc/periodic folders are run on a daily, weekly, and monthly basis by the launchd control process. According to the /System/Library/LaunchDaemons/com.apple. periodic-weekly.plist file, all weekly tasks will be performed at 3:15 a.m. on Saturday mornings. The scripts are run in numeric/ alphabetic order based on their filename. This new script will run last because its name begins with "400."

Use an ARD Task Server to Install Packages

Create a task that will install an installation package on your Client computer the next time that computer becomes available.

1   Disconnect the Ethernet cable on your Client computer.

2   Open Remote Desktop on your server and select your Client computer from the lab1 list.

3   Choose Manage > Install Package from the menu bar.

4   Drag the Rosetta package from Student Materials/Chapter6 folder into the ARD Install Package window.

5   If this package is not available, ask your instructor for directions to the package that you should send to your Client computer.

6   For the "Run this task from" option, select your Task Server.

7   Click Install.

Because your Client computer is currently offline, the task will
remain with the Task Server.

Tasks that can be transferred to a Task Server include install
packages and report information upload.

The main difference between running these tasks from your
local Remote Desktop application and the Task Server is that
the Task Server will automatically retry the task for any target
computers that miss the original scheduled task.

To use Task Server to schedule other tasks, you must create
those tasks directly on the Task Server and schedule their
execution times accordingly.

8   Reconnect the Ethernet cable to your Client computer and
watch the status of the Task Server task change as the installation continues.

9   Once the install is complete, restart the Client computer as
prompted.

Exercise 7.2.4
Update Your Deployment Planning Template

The ongoing monitoring and maintenance of your deployed systems may take many forms. You have been introduced to a handful of techniques that make the upkeep of changes for multiple computers more manageable.

You have several Apple-sourced choices for running repetitive tasks: ARD, Task Server, and launchd. Further, each method may be combined with standard or custom scripts and commands to achieve a high level of automation.

Now it's time to update your template to see which of the various methods demonstrated lend themselves to your particular situation:

- Generating client usage reports via ARD Task Server

- Using your own Software Update server

- Scheduling periodic tasks with launchd

- Scheduling periodic tasks with Task Server

When you fill out your template, please remember to include the rationale for using these forms of deployment.

Answer Key

Chapter 1

None

Chapter 2

Question 1 Did Disk Utility open?

No, Disk Utility did not open. The alias file opens with TextEdit, and garbled text is shown.

Question 2 Did Disk Utility open?

Yes, this time Disk Utility opens.

Question 3 Did the copy succeed?

Yes, there is now enough disk space on the disk image to handle the updated application.

Question 4 Has the size changed?

No.

Question 5 Which of the disk images still works?

Fork1a.dmg still works as it was flattened before using the compression commands.

Chapter 3

Question 1 Will this installation package install successfully?

No, the install fails with a message about not being allowed to install on non-PretendCo computers.

Question 2 Were you able to control the computer?

No, a message is displayed "Authentication failed to "Mac Number"

Question 3 *Were you successful?*

Yes, this time the control function works because the hadmin account is used to contact the client computer.

Chapter 4

Question 1 *Is the hadmin account visible in System Preferences Accounts or in the Fast User Switching menu?*

No, the hadmin account is not visible.

Chapter 5

Question 1 *Did you see a login window on the Client computer?*

No, the Mac OS X install that was restored starts with the Setup Assistant.

Question 2 *Does it have the same customizations as before?*

Some of them, not all.

Question 3 *What is the computer name?*

cadmin's <computer model>

Chapter 6

Question 1 *What new hidden file resides in the /Users folder?*

.PCDS_SetupDone

Question 2 *Did the same installation package get installed again?*

No, a message is displayed saying that

Chapter 7

None